Inspiration from Savitri

Inspiration from Savitri

Art, Architecture

and

the Constructions of Man and God

Vol. 15

By Narad (Richard Eggenberger)

Savitri Foundation

First Edition
15 August 2014

Published by
Savitri Foundation

10, Jorbagh,
New Delhi—110 003
Ph: 011-43001448
E-Mail: info@savitri.in
Website: http://www.savitri.in

Dedication

To Sri Aurobindo, the Seer-Poet and Avatar of the
New Creation, I humbly offer, together with this
volume, my heart and soul in gratitude.

Preface

Sri Aurobindo's epic, Savitri, his Magnum Opus, is replete with splendid images of this and other worlds. In fact, every aspect of human endeavor, human consciousness, human failings, including man's potential, is shown in the clearest detail, possible only by the seer and Avatar of the Supramental.

We must remember also that Sri Aurobindo wrote nothing for 'beauty for beauty's sake, nothing for mere alliteration, imagery, etc. He has written the following in his letters to a disciple/poet.

Here are some passages from his letters about writing Savitri.

"I lay most stress on then are whether each line in itself is the inevitable thing not only as a whole but in each word; whether there is the right distribution of sentence lengths (an immensely important thing in this kind of blank verse); whether the lines are in their right place, for all the lines may be perfect, but they may not combine perfectly together — bridges may be needed, alterations of position so as to create the right development and perspective etc., etc. Pauses hardly exist in this kind of blank verse; variations of rhythm as between the lines, of caesura, of the distribution of long and short, clipped and open syllables, manifold combinations of vowel and consonant sounds, alliteration, assonances, etc., distribution into one line, two line, three or four or five line, many line sentences, care to make each line tell by itself in its own mass and force and at the same time form a harmonious whole sentence — these are the important things. But all that is usually taken care of by the inspiration itself, for as I know and have the habit of the technique, the inspiration provides what I want according to standing orders. If there is a defect I appeal to headquarters till a proper version comes along or the defect is removed by a word or phrase substitute that flashes — with the necessary sound and sense. These things are not done by thinking or seeking for the right thing — the two agents are sight and call. Also feeling — the solar plexus has to be satisfied and, until it is, revision after revision has to continue. I may add that the technique does not go by any set mental rule — for the object is not perfect technical elegance according to precept, but sound-significance filling out word-significance. If that can be done by breaking rules, well, so much the worse for the rule."

Sri Aurobindo writes further:

'Do not forget that the *Savitri* is an experiment in mystic poetry, spiritual poetry cast into a symbolic figure. Done on this scale, it is really a new attempt and cannot be hampered by old ideas of technique except when they are assimilable. Least of all by standards proper to a mere intellectual and abstract poetry which makes "reason and taste" the supreme arbiters, aims at a harmonised poetic-intellectual balanced expression of the sense, elegance in language, a sober and subtle use of imaginative decoration, a restrained emotive element etc. The attempt at mystic spiritual poetry of the kind I am at demands above all a spiritual objectivity, an intense psycho-physical concreteness.'

And lastly:

The mystical poet can only describe what he has felt, seen in himself or others or in the world just as he has felt or seen it or experienced through exact vision, close contact or identity and leave it to the general reader to understand or not understand or misunderstand according to his capacity. A new kind of poetry demands a new mentality in the recipient as well as in the writer.

In this volume, Volume 15, Art and Architecture in Savitri, we look at the many and marvelous ways Sri Aurobindo gives us passages and images of art and architecture.

Please note that all definitions in the Dictionary at the end are taken from the Lexicon of an Infinite Mind, a Dictionary of Words and Terms in Savitri, published by the Savitri Foundation.

We look at the word 'temple' as an example.

temple   **1.** A building or place dedicated to the worship of a deity or deities. **2.** *Fig.* Something regarded as having within it a divine presence.

Across the path of the divine Event
The huge foreboding mind of Night, alone
In her unlit temple of eternity,
Lay stretched immobile upon Silence' marge. ||1.2||

*In the initial lines of Savitri, lines two to five, in the opening canto we see the mind of Night (note the capital 'N') alone in her unlit temple of eternity. One is not only swept up by the beauty of this image but its reverberation continues in the soul. And we see that this 'mind of Night' is in a **temple of eternity,** unlit, no doubt.*

*Let us delight further in passages with the word, **temple,** as it occurs in twenty-four additional passages.*

In this next passage, regarding which a disciple wrote to Sri Aurobindo, asking, "Are not these lines which I regard as the ne plus ultra in world-poetry a snatch of the sheer Overmind?"

Sri Aurobindo replied, in his modest way,

"This passage is, I believe, what I might call the Overmind Intuition at work expressing itself in something like its own rhythm and language. It is difficult to say about one's own poetry, but I think I have succeeded here and in some passages later on in catching that very difficult note; in separate lines or briefer passages (i.e. a few lines at a time) I think it comes in not unoften."

Although the first sentence ends with the word temple, one cannot but quote the entire passage for its transcendent beauty of pure 'Overhead' inspiration.

As in a mystic and dynamic dance
A priestess of immaculate ecstasies
Inspired and ruled from Truth's revealing vault
Moves in some prophet cavern of the gods,
A heart of silence in the hands of joy
Inhabited with rich creative beats
A body like a parable of dawn
That seemed a niche for veiled divinity
Or golden temple door to things beyond. ||3.33||

Immortal rhythms swayed in her time-born steps;
Her look, her smile awoke celestial sense
Even in earth-stuff, and their intense delight
Poured a supernal beauty on men's lives. ||3.34||

A wide self-giving was her native act;
A magnanimity as of sea or sky
Enveloped with its greatness all that came
And gave a sense as of a greatened world:
Her kindly care was a sweet temperate sun,
Her high passion a blue heaven's equipoise. ||3.35||

As might a soul fly like a hunted bird,
Escaping with tired wings from a world of storms,
And a quiet reach like a remembered breast,
In a haven of safety and splendid soft repose
One could drink life back in streams of honey-fire,
Escaping with tired wings from a world of storms,
And a quiet reach like a remembered breast,
In a haven of safety and splendid soft repose
One could drink life back in streams of honey-fire,
Recover the lost habit of happiness,
Feel her bright nature's glorious ambiance,
And preen joy in her warmth and colour's rule. ||3.36||

A deep of compassion, a hushed sanctuary,
Her inward help unbarred a gate in heaven;
Love in her was wider than the universe,
The whole world could take refuge in her single heart. ||3.37||

The great unsatisfied godhead here could dwell:
Vacant of the dwarf self's imprisoned air
Her mood could harbour his sublimer breath
Spiritual that can make all things divine. ||3.38||

For even her gulfs were secrecies of light. ||3.39||

At once she was the stillness and the word,
A continent of self-diffusing peace,
An ocean of untrembling virgin fire:
The strength, the silence of the gods were hers. ||3.40||

*The next instance of temple is especially close to my soul as even when
Sri Aurobindo writes of the darkest experiences in Book Two, he always
lifts us up into the Light.*

This passage exemplifies that uplifting.

Even when we fail to look into our souls
Or lie embedded in earthly consciousness,
Still have we parts that grow towards the Light,
Yet are there luminous tracts and heavens serene
And Eldoradoes of splendour and ecstasy
And temples to the Godhead none can see. ||10.9||

*The next example of the word 'temple' is one that speaks to me of the
structure of the temples of India and here Sri Aurobindo tells us that
the 'inspiring soul of man' builds this tower to 'live near to his dream of
the Invisible.*

So it towered up to heights intangible
And disappeared in the hushed conscious Vast
As climbs a storeyed temple-tower to heaven
Built by the aspiring soul of man to live
Near to his dream of the Invisible. ||26.3||

*In all the great writings of seers and sages the 'temple of the soul'
is prominently featured, but Sri Aurobindo speaks to us of 'Agents of*

darkness', and 'engineers of interest and desire' who build our 'huddled structures of self-will' and with the 'ego's factories and marts' 'surround 'the beautiful temple of the soul'.

Insignificant architects of low-built lives
And engineers of interest and desire,
Out of crude earthiness and muddy thrills
And coarse reactions of material nerve
They build our huddled structures of self-will
And the ill-lighted mansions of our thought,
Or with the ego's factories and marts
Surround the beautiful temple of the soul. ||45.25||

In this this passage Aswapathy is in the <u>Kingdoms and Godheads of the Greater Life</u> *and there...*

All powers of Life towards their godhead tend
In the wideness and the daring of that air,
Each builds its temple and expands its cult,
And Sin too there is a divinity. ||51.21||

In Canto VIII of Book Two, when Sri Aurobindo (Aswapathy) descends to find The World of Falsehood, the Mother of Evil and the Sons of Darkness he sees that these artificers, those skilled or clever in devising ways of making things, have built their altars 'in the clay temple of terrestrial life', our human ground, perhaps even in some, the human body.

Adepts of the illusion and the mask,
The artificers of Nature's fall and pain
Have built their altars of triumphant Night
In the clay temple of terrestrial life. ||63.8||

However, in Book II, Canto XII, The Heavens of the Ideal, he sees that there is a 'deathless Rose' between and behind our life, and its bud is born in us and somehow, 'by a touch, a presence or a voice' our world becomes a temple ground.

Here too its bud is born in human breasts;
Then by a touch, a presence or a voice
The world is turned into a temple ground
And all discloses the unknown Beloved. ||73.10||

*In Book II, Canto XIV, Aswapathy is led by a mysterious sound, that is
all sounds in turn and at one point seems like 'the solemn reminder of
a temple gong' It is a passage that I often read to the OM Choirs as all
sounds ultimately merge into one, OM.*

*In Book III, The Book of the Divine Mother, Canto III, The House of the
Spirit and the New Creation, we are shown a world of beauty and joy
and are given glimpses of the New Creation and find that*

"In the temple of the idea shrined the One:"

In Book IV, Canto II, Sri Aurobindo speaks of Savitri and her heart...

Thus was it for a while with Savitri,
All worshipped marvellingly, none dared to claim. ||97.11||

Her mind sat high pouring its golden beams,
Her heart was a crowded temple of delight. ||97.12||

*One could go on and on selecting word after word and passage after
passage to learn all that Savitri contains within its pages and is the
vision and the promise of the future of earth and man.*

*I remember the time in 1961 when I first met Mother. In an instant
my life was changed forever. Living in the Ashram I met great yogi's
who were following the path of the Integral Yoga. I also met seekers
from many parts of the world. On one occasion I was given a copy of
The Odyssey by Kazantzakis, a work of 33,000 lines, translated into
English from the Greek. I marvelled at the beauty of his imagery, the
multitudinous descriptions of the sun, and his poetic genius. Then I was
given a copy of Savitri and never picked up the Odyssey again because
all I needed to progress on the path of Integral Yoga could be found
within its pages.*

Acknowledgements

To RY Deshpande whose life's dedication to Savitri continues to enlighten seekers with his vast understanding. It is he who encouraged me to write this series of volumes, *Inspiration from Savitri*. I am ever grateful for his generous assistance in enabling them to be published under the auspices of the Savitri Foundation.

To Narendra for his devotion to Savitri and the unstinting assistance he has given me, his artwork, his excellent guidance and his generosity.

To all who love Savitri and find through it the inspiration to aspire to a higher and truer life.

Publishers' Note

Savitri Foundation considers it a privilege to bring out a series of books under the title *Inspiration from Savitri* edited by Narad (Richard Eggenberger). We are thankful to the author for enthusiastically participating in this significant venture.

Guide to Indexing of Sentences

The indexing is based on the *Digital-friendly* Edition of *Savitri* published by Savitri Foundation

||5.40|| 40th Sentence in the 5th Running Section of the whole Epic

Example:

Out of apprenticeship to Ignorance
Wisdom upraised him to her master craft
And made him an arch-mason of the soul,
A builder of the Immortal's secret house,
An aspirant to supernal Timelessness:
Freedom and empire called to him from on high;
Above mind's twilight and life's star-led night
There gleamed the dawn of a spiritual day. ||5.40||

For quick web access to sentences just append the sentence index to url:

http://savitri.in/read/

So that our example sentence will have the url:

http://savitri.in/read/5.40

Contents

Man the Builder

Design and Construction of God and Man

**Art and Artistry, The Designs of God,
Man and other powers.**

The Architect and Builder

arch-mason

Out of apprenticeship to Ignorance
Wisdom upraised him to her master craft
And made him an arch-mason of the soul,
A builder of the Immortal's secret house,
An aspirant to supernal Timelessness:
Freedom and empire called to him from on high;
Above mind's twilight and life's star-led night
There gleamed the dawn of a spiritual day. ||5.40||

In this drop from consciousness to consciousness
Each leaned on the occult Inconscient's power,
The fountain of its needed Ignorance,
Archmason of the limits by which it lives. ||24.5||

Arch-masons of the eternal Thaumaturge,
Moulders and measurers of fragmented space,
They have made their plan of the concealed and known
A dwelling-house for the invisible King. ||71.11||

It is an architecture high and grand
By many named and nameless masons built
In which unseeing hands obey the Unseen,
And of its master-builders she is one. ||112.42||

Earth is the chosen place of mightiest souls;
Earth is the heroic spirit's battlefield,
The forge where the Arch-mason shapes his works. ||151.4||

architect

The immobile lips, the great surreal wings,
The visage masked by superconscient Sleep,
The eyes with their closed lids that see all things,
Appeared of the Architect who builds in trance. ||8.21||

Insignificant architects of low-built lives
And engineers of interest and desire,
Out of crude earthiness and muddy thrills
And coarse reactions of material nerve
They build our huddled structures of self-will
And the ill-lighted mansions of our thought,
Or with the ego's factories and marts
Surround the beautiful temple of the soul. ||45.25||

The Anarchs of the formless depths arose,
Great titan beings and demoniac powers,
World-egos racked with lust and thought and will,
Vast minds and lives without a spirit within:
Impatient architects of error's house,
Leaders of the cosmic ignorance and unrest
And sponsors of sorrow and mortality
Embodied the dark Ideas of the Abyss. ||61.5||

A twilight sage whose shadow seems to him Self,
Moving from minute to brief minute lives;
A king dependent on his satellites
Signs the decrees of ignorant ministers,
A judge in half-possession of his proofs,
A voice clamant of uncertainty's postulates,
An architect of knowledge, not its source. ||66.18||

High architects of possibility
And engineers of the impossible,
Mathematicians of the infinitudes
And theoricians of unknowable truths,
They formulate enigma's postulates
And join the unknown to the apparent worlds. ||71.27||

There was nothing there but a schema drawn by sense,
A substitute for eternal mysteries,
A scrawl figure of reality, a plan
And elevation by the architect Word
Imposed upon the semblances of Time. ||74.28||

An architect hewing out self's living rock,
Phenomenon built Reality's summer-house
On the beaches of the sea of Infinity. ||86.29||

I saw them cross the twilight of an age,
The sun-eyed children of a marvellous dawn,
The great creators with wide brows of calm,
The massive barrier-breakers of the world
And wrestlers with destiny in her lists of will,
The labourers in the quarries of the gods,
The messengers of the Incommunicable,
The architects of immortality. ||90.29||

A prescient architect of Fate and Chance
Who builds our lives on a foreseen design
The meaning knows and consequence of each step
And watches the inferior stumbling powers. ||99.13||

This world was not built with random bricks of chance,
A blind god is not destiny's architect;
A conscious power has drawn the plan of life,
There is a meaning in each curve and line. ||112.41||

In him the architect of the visible world,
At once the art and artist of his works,
Spirit and seer and thinker of things seen,
Virât, who lights his camp-fires in the suns
And the star-entangled ether is his hold,
Expressed himself with Matter for his speech:
Objects are his letters, forces are his words,
Events are the crowded history of his life,
And sea and land are the pages of his tale,
Matter is his means and his spiritual sign;
He hangs the thought upon a lash's lift,
In the current of the blood makes flow the soul. ||149.15||

architecture

A crown of the architecture of the worlds,
A mystery of married Earth and Heaven
Annexed divinity to the mortal scheme. ||5.34||

In an architecture of hieratic Space
Circling and mounting towards creation's tops,
At a blue height which never was too high
For warm communion between body and soul,
As far as heaven, as near as thought and hope,
Glimmered the kingdom of a griefless life. ||33.3||

A sovereign ruling falsehood, death and grief,
It pressed its fierce hegemony on earth;
Disharmonising the original style
Of the architecture of her fate's design,
It falsified the primal cosmic Will
And bound to struggle and dread vicissitudes
The long slow process of the patient Power. ||62.11||

Apt to conceive, unable to attain,
It drew its concept-maps and vision-plans
Too large for the architecture of mortal Space. ||69.5||

The architecture of the Infinite
Discovered here its inward-musing shapes
Captured into wide breadths of soaring stone:
Music brought down celestial yearnings, song
Held the merged heart absorbed in rapturous depths,
Linking the human with the cosmic cry;
The world-interpreting movements of the dance
Moulded idea and mood to a rhythmic sway
And posture; crafts minute in subtle lines
Eternised a swift moment's memory
Or showed in a carving's sweep, a cup's design
The underlying patterns of the unseen:
Poems in largeness cast like moving worlds
And metres surging with the ocean's voice
Translated by grandeurs locked in Nature's heart
But thrown now into a crowded glory of speech
The beauty and sublimity of her forms,
The passion of her moments and her moods
Lifting the human word near to the god's. ||95.13||

It is an architecture high and grand
By many named and nameless masons built
In which unseeing hands obey the Unseen,
And of its master-builders she is one. ||112.42||

Look on these forms that stay awhile and pass,
These lives that long and strive, then are no more,
These structures that have no abiding truth,
The saviour creeds that cannot save themselves,
But perish in the strangling hands of the years,
Discarded from man's thought, proved false by Time,
Philosophies that strip all problems bare
But nothing ever have solved since earth began,
And sciences omnipotent in vain
By which men learn of what the suns are made,
Transform all forms to serve their outward needs,

Ride through the sky and sail beneath the sea,
But learn not what they are or why they came;
These polities, architectures of man's brain,
That, bricked with evil and good, wall in man's spirit
And, fissured houses, palace at once and jail,
Rot while they reign and crumble before they crash;
These revolutions, demon or drunken god,
Convulsing the wounded body of mankind
Only to paint in new colours an old face;
These wars, carnage triumphant, ruin gone mad,
The work of centuries vanishing in an hour,
The blood of the vanquished and the victor's crown
Which men to be born must pay for with their pain,
The hero's face divine on satyr's limbs,
The demon's grandeur mixed with the demi-god's,
The glory and the beasthood and the shame;
Why is it all, the labour and the din,
The transient joys, the timeless sea of tears,
The longing and the hoping and the cry,
The battle and the victory and the fall,
The aimless journey that can never pause,
The waking toil, the incoherent sleep? ||144.14||

builder

Out of apprenticeship to Ignorance
Wisdom upraised him to her master craft
And made him an arch-mason of the soul,
A builder of the Immortal's secret house,
An aspirant to supernal Timelessness:
Freedom and empire called to him from on high;
Above mind's twilight and life's star-led night
There gleamed the dawn of a spiritual day. ||5.40||

Abandoned to her rapid fancy's moods
And the rich coloured riot of her mind,

Initiate of divine and mighty dreams,
Magician builder of unnumbered forms
Exploring the measures of the rhythms of God,
At will she wove her wizard wonder-dance,
A Dionysian goddess of delight,
A Bacchant of creative ecstasy. ||35.50||

There is kept grandeur's store, the hero's mould;
The soul is the watchful builder of its fate;
None is a spirit indifferent and inert;
They choose their side, they see the god they adore. ||51.15||

Assailed by the edge of the convicting beam
The builder Reason lost her confidence
In the successful sleight and turn of thought
That makes the soul the prisoner of a phrase. ||74.26||

How long shall our spirits battle with the Night
And bear defeat and the brute yoke of Death,
We who are vessels of a deathless Force
And builders of the godhead of the race? ||90.5||

It is an architecture high and grand
By many named and nameless masons built
In which unseeing hands obey the Unseen,
And of its master-builders she is one. ||112.42||

Death bowed his head in scornful cold assent,
The builder of this dreamlike earth for man
Who has mocked with vanity all gifts he gave. ||137.64||

This is the stuff from which the ideal is formed:
Its builder is thought, its base the heart's desire,
But nothing real answers to their call. ||140.6||

A huge inhuman Cyclopean voice,
A Babel-builder's song towering to heaven,
A throb of engines and the clang of tools
Brought the deep undertone of labour's pain. ||143.8||

Impeccable artists of unerring forms,
Magician builders of sound and rhythmic words,
Wind-haired Gundhurvas chanted to the ear
The odes that shape the universal thought,
The lines that tear the veil from Deity's face,
The rhythms that bring the sounds of wisdom's sea. ||148.42||

The altar

I do not believe that anywhere in all the poetry and literature of humanity one will find the brilliance of Sri Aurobindo's use of the word 'altar'. We have 'altar hills', 'altar Mind' , the 'altar's plan', the 'heart's altar' and so much more that we are left speechless at the beauty and force of these passages.

Air was a vibrant link between earth and heaven;
The wide-winged hymn of a great priestly wind
Arose and failed upon the altar hills;
The high boughs prayed in a revealing sky. ||1.35||

The restless nether members tire of peace;
A nostalgia of old little works and joys,
A need to call back small familiar selves,
To tread the accustomed and inferior way,
The need to rest in a natural poise of fall,
As a child who learns to walk can walk not long,
Replace the titan will for ever to climb,
On the heart's altar dim the sacred fire. ||7.3||

But vain unending is the sacrifice,
The priest an ignorant mage who only makes
Futile mutations in the altar's plan
And casts blind hopes into a powerless flame. ||37.22||

A mastering virtue statuesques the pose,
Or a titan passion goads to a proud unrest:
At Wisdom's altar they are kings and priests
Or their life a sacrifice to an idol of Power. ||51.24||

In high professions wrapped self-will walked wide
And licence stalked prating of order and right:
There was no altar raised to Liberty;
True freedom was abhorred and hunted down:
Harmony and tolerance nowhere could be seen;
Each group proclaimed its dire and naked Law. ||57.6||

A servile blinkered silence hushed the mind
Or only it repeated lessons taught,
While mitred, holding the good shepherd's staff,
Falsehood enthroned on awed and prostrate hearts
The cults and creeds that organise living death
And slay the soul on the altar of a lie. ||59.13||

A shadow fell across the simple Ray:
Obscured was the Truth-light in the cavern heart
That burns unwitnessed in the altar crypt
Behind the still velamen's secrecy
Companioning the Godhead of the shrine. ||62.13||

Adepts of the illusion and the mask,
The artificers of Nature's fall and pain
Have built their altars of triumphant Night
In the clay temple of terrestrial life. ||63.8||

A bright Error fringed the mystery-altar's frieze;
Darkness grew nurse to wisdom's occult sun,
Myth suckled knowledge with her lustrous milk;
The infant passed from dim to radiant breasts. ||66.37||

In a veiled Nature's hallowed secrecies
It burns for ever on the altar Mind,
Its priests the souls of dedicated gods,
Humanity its house of sacrifice. ||73.24||

Our human knowledge is a candle burnt
On a dim altar to a sun-vast Truth;
Man's virtue, a coarse-spun ill-fitting dress,
Apparels wooden images of Good;
Passionate and blinded, bleeding, stained with mire
His energy stumbles towards a deathless Force. ||73.32||

Upward it rose to grasp the human scene:
The strong Inhabitant turned to watch her field,
A lovelier light assumed her spirit brow
And sweet and solemn grew her musing gaze;
Celestial-human deep warm slumbrous fires
Woke in the long fringed glory of her eyes
Like altar-burnings in a mysteried shrine. ||94.92||

All her life's turns led her to symbol doors
Admitting to secret Powers that were her kin;
Adept of truth, initiate of bliss,
A mystic acolyte trained in Nature's school,
Aware of the marvel of created things
She laid the secrecies of her heart's deep muse
Upon the altar of the Wonderful;
Her hours were ritual in a timeless fane;
Her acts became gestures of sacrifice. ||95.8||

A goddess in a net of inconscience caught,
Self-bound in the pastures of death she dreams of life,
Self-racked with the pains of hell aspires to joy,
And builds to hope her altars of despair,
Knows that one high step might enfranchise all
And, suffering, looks for greatness in her sons. ||98.18||

He turns for little gains to ignorant Powers
Or kindles his altar lights to a demon face. ||98.20||

Muse-lipped she nursed her symbol mysteries
And guarded for her pure-eyed sacraments
The valley-clefts between her breasts of joy,
Her mountain-altars for the fires of dawn
And nuptial beaches where the ocean couched
And the huge chanting of her prophet woods. ||99.28||

On the altar throwing thy thoughts, thy heart, thy works,
Thy fate is a long sacrifice to the gods   Berenley
Till they have opened to thee thy secret self
And made thee one with the indwelling God. ||112.32

At first to her beneath the sapphire heavens
The sylvan solitude was a gorgeous dream,
An altar of the summer's splendour and fire,
A sky-topped flower-hung palace of the gods
And all its scenes a smile on rapture's lips
And all its voices bards of happiness. ||115.1||

These she controlled, nothing was shown outside:
She was still to them the child they knew and loved;
The sorrowing woman they saw not within;
No change was in her beautiful motions seen:
A worshipped empress all once vied to serve,

She made herself the diligent serf of all,
Nor spared the labour of broom and jar and well,
Or close gentle tending or to heap the fire
Of altar and kitchen, no slight task allowed
To others that her woman's strength might do. ||115.22||

Thus in the silent chamber of her soul
Cloistering her love to live with secret grief
She dwelt like a dumb priest with hidden gods
Unappeased by the wordless offering of her days,
Lifting to them her sorrow like frankincense,
Her life the altar, herself the sacrifice. ||115.41||

Around her body's stillness all grew still:
Her heart listened to its slow measured beats,
Her mind renouncing thought heard and was mute:
"Why camest thou to this dumb deathbound earth,
This ignorant life beneath indifferent skies
Tied like a sacrifice on the altar of Time,
O spirit, O immortal energy,
If 'twas to nurse grief in a helpless heart
Or with hard tearless eyes awake thy doom? ||116.5||

For only there could dwell the soul's firm truth:
Imperishable, a tongue of sacrifice,
It flamed unquenched upon the central hearth
Where burns for the high house-lord and his mate
The homestead's sentinel and witness fire
From which the altars of the gods are lit. ||142.104||

apse

In darkling aisles with evil eyes for lamps
And fatal voices chanting from the apse,
In strange infernal dim basilicas

Intoning the magic of the unholy Word,
The ominous profound Initiate
Performed the ritual of her mysteries. ||61.12||

basilicas

In darkling aisles with evil eyes for lamps
And fatal voices chanting from the apse,
In strange infernal dim basilicas
Intoning the magic of the unholy Word,
The ominous profound Initiate
Performed the ritual of her mysteries. ||61.12||

cathedral

Here too, the word cathedral is found four times in Savitri yet not
once as the structure. The last passage is especially beautiful as Sri
Aurobindo uses the word as a verb. To cathedral light, to contain or hold
light as in a cathedral, an exceptional and extraordinary image seen and
experienced by the avatar and seer-poet.

Impassive he lived immune from earthly hopes,
A figure in the ineffable Witness' shrine
Pacing the vast cathedral of his thoughts
Under its arches dim with infinity
And heavenward brooding of invisible wings. ||20.4||

Adorer of a joy without a name,
In her obscure cathedral of delight
To dim dwarf gods she offers secret rites. ||31.21||

Escaped from surface sight and mortal sense
The seizing harmony of its shapes became
The strange significant icon of a Power
Renewing its inscrutable descent
Into a human figure of its works

That stood out in life's bold abrupt relief
On the soil of the evolving universe,
A godhead sculptured on a wall of thought,
Mirrored in the flowing hours and dimly shrined
In Matter as in a cathedral cave. ||98.37||

This was the aim, this the supernal Law,
Nature's allotted task when beauty-drenched
In dim mist waters of inconscient sleep,
Out of the Void this grand creation rose,—
For this the Spirit came into the Abyss
And charged with its power Matter's unknowing Force,
In Night's bare session to cathedral light
In Death's realm repatriate immortality. ||142.19||

chapel

In a fell chapel of iniquity
To worship a black pitiless image of Power
Kneeling one must cross hard-hearted stony courts,
A pavement like a floor of evil fate. ||64.12||

He stood erect, a Godlike form and force
And a soul's thoughts looked out from earthborn eyes;
Man stood erect, he wore the thinker's brow:
He looked at heaven and saw his comrade stars;
A vision came of beauty and greater birth
Slowly emerging from the heart's chapel of light
And moved in a white lucent air of dreams. ||117.82||

chariot

Since Savitri is travelling in a chariot we expect to read physical
descriptions of it but again, Sri Aurobindo opens us to much more, as in
the scintillating line, 'O traveller in the chariot of the Sun, and the lines
about the chariots of the Gods. Here is vision and yogic experience at
the height of poetic brilliance.

There walled apart by its own innerness
In a mystical barrage of dynamic light
He saw a lone immense high-curved world-pile
Erect like a mountain chariot of the Gods
Motionless under an inscrutable sky. ||26.1||

Immutable in rhythmic calm and joy
He saw, sovereignly free in limitless light,
The unfallen planes, the thought-created worlds
Where Knowledge is the leader of the act
And Matter is of thinking substance made,
Feeling, a heaven-bird poised on dreaming wings,
Answers Truth's call as to a parent's voice,
Form luminous leaps from the all-shaping beam
And Will is a conscious chariot of the Gods,
And Life, a splendour-stream of musing Force,
Carries the voices of the mystic Suns. ||70.32||

A chariot of the marvels of the heavens
Broad-based to bear the gods on fiery wheels,
Flaming he swept through the spiritual gates. ||92.9||

At first her path ran far through peopled tracts:
Admitted to the lion eye of States
And theatres of the loud act of man,
Her carven chariot with its fretted wheels
Threaded through clamorous marts and sentinel towers
Past figured gates and high dream-sculptured fronts
And gardens hung in the sapphire of the skies,
Pillared assembly halls with armoured guards,
Small fanes where one calm Image watched man's life
And temples hewn as if by exiled gods
To imitate their lost eternity. ||99.16||

Here was the childhood of primeval earth,
Here timeless musings large and glad and still,
Men had forborne as yet to fill with cares,
Imperial acres of the eternal sower
And wind-stirred grass-lands winking in the sun:
Or mid green musing of woods and rough-browed hills,
In the grove's murmurous bee-air humming wild
Or past the long lapsing voice of silver floods
Like a swift hope journeying among its dreams
Hastened the chariot of the golden bride. ||99.20||

Hooves trampling fast, wheels largely stumbling ceased;
The chariot stood like an arrested wind. ||102.33||

Aimless man toils in an uncertain world
Lulled by inconstant pauses of his pain,
Scourged like a beast by the infinite desire,
Bound to the chariot of the dreadful gods. ||137.48||

O traveller in the chariot of the Sun,
High priestess in the holy fancy's shrine
Who with a magic ritual in earth's house
Worshippest ideal and eternal love,
What is this love thy thought has deified,
This sacred legend and immortal myth? ||140.28||

In thee the secret sight man's blindness missed
Has opened its view past Time, my chariot course,
And death, my tunnel which I drive through life
To reach my unseen distances of bliss. ||150.2||

I will pour delight from thee as from a jar,
I will whirl thee as my chariot through the ways,
I will use thee as my sword and as my lyre,
I will play on thee my minstrelsies of thought. ||154.37||

Now mind is all and its uncertain ray,
Mind is the leader of the body and life,
Mind the thought-driven chariot of the soul
Carrying the luminous wanderer in the night
To vistas of a far uncertain dawn,
To the end of the Spirit's fathomless desire,
To its dream of absolute truth and utter bliss. ||155.13||

citadel

In the malignant hollows of the world,
In its subconscient cavern-passages
Ambushed they lie waiting their hour to leap,
Surrounding with danger the sieged city of life:
Admitted into the citadel of man's days
They mine his force and maim or suddenly kill. ||107.21||

colonnade

The past receded and the future neared:
Far now behind lay Madra's spacious halls,
The white carved pillars, the cool dim alcoves,
The tinged mosaic of the crystal floors,
The towered pavilions, the wind-rippled pools
And gardens humming with the murmur of bees,
Forgotten soon or a pale memory
The fountain's plash in the wide stone-bound pool,
The thoughtful noontide's brooding solemn trance,
The colonnade's dream grey in the quiet eve,
The slow moonrise gliding in front of Night. ||114.10||

cornices

Flames of self-lost immobile reverie,
Doves crowded the grey musing cornices
Like sculptured postures of white-bosomed peace. ||125.25||

cottage

Once more she was human upon earthly soil
In the muttering night amid the rain-swept woods
And the rude cottage where she sat in trance:
That subtle world withdrew deeply within
Behind the sun-veil of the inner sight. ||127.1||

dwelling

Each time he rose there was a larger poise,
A dwelling on a higher spirit plane;
The Light remained in him a longer space. ||7.13||

Only the Immortals on their deathless heights
Dwelling beyond the walls of Time and Space,
Masters of living, free from the bonds of Thought,
Who are overseers of Fate and Chance and Will
And experts of the theorem of world-need,
Can see the Idea, the Might that change Time's course,
Come maned with light from undiscovered worlds,
Hear, while the world toils on with its deep blind heart,
The galloping hooves of the unforeseen event,
Bearing the superhuman rider, near
And, impassive to earth's din and startled cry,
Return to the silence of the hills of God;
As lightning leaps, as thunder sweeps, they pass
And leave their mark on the trampled breast of Life. ||11.38||

The Ideal must be Nature's common truth,
The body illumined with the indwelling God,
The heart and mind feel one with all that is,
A conscious soul live in a conscious world. ||19.4||

As when a search-light stabs the Night's blind breast
And dwellings and trees and figures of men appear
As if revealed to an eye in Nothingness,

All lurking things were torn out of their veils
And held up in his vision's sun-white blaze. ||43.5||

This seeming driver of her wheel of works
Missioned to motive and record her drift
And fix its law on her inconstant powers,
This master-spring of a delicate enginery,
Aspired to enlighten its user and refine
Lifting to a vision of the indwelling Power
The absorbed mechanic's crude initiative:
He raised his eyes; Heaven-light mirrored a Face. ||44.35||

It loves the old ground that was its dwelling-place:
Abhorring change as an audacious sin,
Distrustful of each new discovery
Only it advances step by careful step
And fears as if a deadly abyss the unknown. ||68.7||

Arch-masons of the eternal Thaumaturge,
Moulders and measurers of fragmented space,
They have made their plan of the concealed and known
A dwelling-house for the invisible King. ||71.11||

Why is thy dwelling in the pathless wood
Far from the deeds thy glorious youth demands,
Haunt of the anchorites and earth's wilder broods,
Where only with thy witness self thou roam'st
In Nature's green unhuman loneliness
Surrounded by enormous silences
And the blind murmur of primeval calms?" ||103.23||

I strove to find its hints through Beauty and Art,
But Form cannot unveil the indwelling Power;
Only it throws its symbols at our hearts. ||103.64||

To her own despair answer the mother made;
As one she cried who in her heavy heart
Labours amid the sobbing of her hopes
To wake a note of help from sadder strings;
"O child, in the magnificence of thy soul
Dwelling on the border of a greater world,
And, dazzled by thy superhuman thoughts,
Thou lendst eternity to a mortal hope. ||106.167||

On the altar throwing thy thoughts, thy heart, thy works,
Thy fate is a long sacrifice to the gods
Till they have opened to thee thy secret self
And made thee one with the indwelling God. ||112.32||

Our larger being sits behind cryptic walls:
There are greatnesses hidden in our unseen parts
That wait their hour to step into life's front:
We feel an aid from deep indwelling Gods:
One speaks within, Light comes to us from above. ||117.75||

As if an old remembered dream come true,
She recognised in her prophetic mind
The imperishable lustre of that sky,
The tremulous sweetness of that happy air
And, covered from mind's view and life's approach,
The mystic cavern in the sacred hill
And knew the dwelling of her secret soul. ||125.19||

But higher still can climb the ascending light;
There are vasts of vision and eternal suns,
Oceans of an immortal luminousness,
Flame-hills assaulting heaven with their peaks,
There dwelling all becomes a blaze of sight;
A burning head of vision leads the mind,
Thought trails behind it its long comet tail;

The heart glows, an illuminate and seer,
And sense is kindled into identity. ||146.51||

A halo of the indwelling Deity,
The Immortal's lustre that had lit her face
And tented its radiance in her body's house,
Overflowing made the air a luminous sea. ||147.4||

There breath carried a stream of seeing mind,
Form was a tenuous raiment of the soul:
Colour was a visible tone of ecstasy;
Shapes seen half immaterial by the gaze
And yet voluptuously palpable
Made sensible to touch the indwelling spirit.

For it is given back, but it is known,
A playing ground and dwelling house of God
Who hides himself in bird and beast and man
Sweetly to find himself again by love,
By oneness. His presence leads the rhythms of life
That seek for mutual joy in spite of pain. ||157.45||

fane

All her life's turns led her to symbol doors
Admitting to secret Powers that were her kin;
Adept of truth, initiate of bliss,
A mystic acolyte trained in Nature's school,
Aware of the marvel of created things
She laid the secrecies of her heart's deep muse
Upon the altar of the Wonderful;
Her hours were ritual in a timeless fane; (Temple)
Her acts became gestures of sacrifice. ||95.8||

At first her path ran far through peopled tracts:
Admitted to the lion eye of States

And theatres of the loud act of man,
Her carven chariot with its fretted wheels
Threaded through clamorous marts and sentinel towers
Past figured gates and high dream-sculptured fronts
And gardens hung in the sapphire of the skies,
Pillared assembly halls with armoured guards,
Small fanes where one calm Image watched man's life
And temples hewn as if by exiled gods
To imitate their lost eternity. ||99.16||

Unknown to himself lives a hidden king
Behind rich tapestries in great secret rooms;
An epicure of the spirit's unseen joys,
He lives on the sweet honey of solitude:
A nameless god in an unapproachable fane,
In the secret adytum of his inmost soul
He guards the being's covered mysteries
Beneath the threshold behind shadowy gates
Or shut in vast cellars of inconscient sleep. ||117.19||

fountain

Yes, the physical fountains are there at the palace of King Aswapathy and his queen but here once more we marvel at Sri Aurobindo's use of words and phrases, expanding the English language through his universal vision as no one has done since the time of Shakespeare and through the power of the mantra surpassing Shakespeare.

We cannot utter, even in hushed tones, enough praise for lines such as:

'O radiant fountain of the world's delight"

Yet we cannot catch the essence of these passages alone, though they stir us in our depths, unless we read further, so these 'Inspiration" volumes serve only as a gateway to the joy one will experience reading

Savitri, in which is contained the key to the New World, the New
Consciousness and the New Man.

A treasure of honey in the combs of God,
A Splendour burning in a tenebrous cloak,
It is our glory of the flame of God,
Our golden fountain of the world's delight,
An immortality cowled in the cape of death,
The shape of our unborn divinity. ||10.27||

In this drop from consciousness to consciousness
Each leaned on the occult Inconscient's power,
The fountain of its needed Ignorance,
Archmason of the limits by which it lives. ||24.5||

O radiant fountain of the world's delight
World-free and unattainable above,
O Bliss who ever dwellst deep hid within
While men seek thee outside and never find,
Mystery and Muse with hieratic tongue,
Incarnate the white passion of thy force,
Mission to earth some living form of thee. ||90.37||

The past receded and the future neared:
Far now behind lay Madra's spacious halls,
The white carved pillars, the cool dim alcoves,
The tinged mosaic of the crystal floors,
The towered pavilions, the wind-rippled pools
And gardens humming with the murmur of bees,
Forgotten soon or a pale memory
The fountain's plash in the wide stone-bound pool,
The thoughtful noontide's brooding solemn trance,
The colonnade's dream grey in the quiet eve,
The slow moonrise gliding in front of Night. ||114.10||

Immortal leader of her mortality,
Doer of her works and fountain of her words,
Invulnerable by Time, omnipotent,
It stood above her calm, immobile, mute. ||134.23||

In her beginningless infinity
Through her soul's reaches unconfined she gazed;
She saw the undying fountains of her life,
She knew herself eternal without birth. ||137.34||

frieze

A bright Error fringed the mystery-altar's frieze;
Darkness grew nurse to wisdom's occult sun,
Myth suckled knowledge with her lustrous milk;
The infant passed from dim to radiant breasts. ||66.37||

A march of friezes marked the lowest steps;
Fantastically ornate and richly small,
They had room for the whole meaning of a world,
Symbols minute of its perfection's joy,
Strange beasts that were Nature's forces made alive
And, wakened to the wonder of his role,
Man grown an image undefaced of God
And objects the fine coin of Beauty's reign;
But wide the terrains were those levels serve. ||71.9||

habitation

As if a music old yet ever new,
Moving suggestions on her heart-strings dwelt,
Thoughts that no habitation found, yet clung
With passionate repetition to her mind,
Desires that hurt not, happy only to live
Always the same and always unfulfilled
Sang in the breast like a celestial lyre. ||139.22||

home, homeland, homeless, homestead

Where is our home? Is it a physical place or something beyond these temporal bodies. Is our home in a world beyond this terrestrial existence, in some far-off heavenly home or is it in the bosom of the Divine. Or do we live in eternity? . There are the homes of the Gods, and homes in all the realms that Aswapathy passes through. Every nuance, every sign, every meaning of home is giving to us in Savitri in passage after passage that we may dwell on the truth of our lives and the future of our earth.

As if solicited in an alien world
With timid and hazardous instinctive grace,
Orphaned and driven out to seek a home,
An errant marvel with no place to live,
Into a far-off nook of heaven there came
A slow miraculous gesture's dim appeal. ||1.19||

In her he found a vastness like his own,
His high warm subtle ether he refound
And moved in her as in his natural home. ||3.41||

He saw the Perfect in their starry homes
Wearing the glory of a deathless form
Lain in the arms of the Eternal's peace,
Rapt in the heart-beats of God-ecstasy. ||6.17||

There knowledge needs not words to embody Idea;
Idea seeking a house in boundlessness,
Weary of its homeless immortality,
Asks not in thought's carved brilliant cell to rest
Whose single window's clipped outlook on things
Sees only a little arc of God's vast sky. ||6.48||

For into the ignorant nature's gusty field,
Into the half-ordered chaos of mortal life
The formless Power, the Self of eternal light
Follow in the shadow of the spirit's descent;
The twin duality for ever one
Chooses its home mid the tumults of the sense. ||7.6||

Already in him was seen that task of Power:
Life made its home on the high tops of self;
His soul, mind, heart became a single sun;
Only life's lower reaches remained dim. ||7.23||

As one forgetting he searches for himself;
As if he had lost an inner light he seeks:
As a sojourner lingering amid alien scenes
He journeys to a home he knows no more. ||16.5||

The glory he had glimpsed must be his home. ||19.2||

In this soar from consciousness to consciousness
Each lifted tops to That from which it came,
Origin of all that it had ever been
And home of all that it could still become. ||24.6||

Affranchised from the net of earthly sense
Calm continents of potency were glimpsed;
Homelands of beauty shut to human eyes,
Half-seen at first through wonder's gleaming lids,
Surprised the vision with felicity;
Sunbelts of knowledge, moonbelts of delight
Stretched out in an ecstasy of widenesses
Beyond our indigent corporeal range. ||24.22||

A Nature lifted by a larger breath,
Plastic and passive to the all-shaping Fire,
Answers the flaming Godhead's casual touch:
Immune from our inertia of response
It hears the word to which our hearts are deaf,
Adopts the seeing of immortal eyes
And, traveller on the roads of line and hue,
Pursues the spirit of beauty to its home. ||30.31||

In us too the intuitive Fire can burn;
An agent Light, it is coiled in our folded hearts,
On the celestial levels is its home:
Descending, it can bring those heavens here. ||3036||

A vagrancy was there that brooked no home,
A journey of countless paths without a close. ||32.5||

Yet pure and bright from the Timeless was her birth,
A lost world-rapture lingers in her eyes,
Her moods are faces of the Infinite:
Beauty and happiness are her native right,
And endless bliss is her eternal home. ||32.23||

A fierier sense had there its home,
A burning urge no earthly limbs can hold. ||35.10||

There were realms where Knowledge joined creative Power
In her high home and made her all his own:
The grand Illuminate seized her gleaming limbs
And filled them with the passion of his ray
Till all her body was its transparent house
And all her soul a counterpart of his soul. ||35.24||

As comes a goddess to a mortal's breast
And fills his days with her celestial clasp,
She stooped to make her home in transient shapes;
In Matter's womb she cast the Immortal's fire,
In the unfeeling Vast woke thought and hope,
Smote with her charm and beauty flesh and nerve
And forced delight on earth's insensible frame. ||36.18||

Ardent from the sack of happy peaceful homes
And gorged with slaughter, plunder, rape and fire,
They made of human selves their helpless prey,
A drove of captives led to lifelong woe
Or torture a spectacle made and holiday,
Mocking or thrilled by their torn victim's pangs;
Admiring themselves as titans and as gods
Proudly they sang their high and glorious deeds
And praised their victory and their splendid force. ||41.21||

Our life's uncertain way winds circling on,
Our mind's unquiet search asks always light,
Till they have learnt their secret in their source,
In the light of the Timeless and its spaceless home,
In the joy of the Eternal sole and one. ||43.24||

A child of heaven who never saw his home,
Its impetus meets the eternal at a point:
It can only near and touch, it cannot hold;
It can only strain towards some bright extreme:
Its greatness is to seek and to create. ||50.36||

Alone the God-given hymn escapes her art
That came with her from her spiritual home
But stopped half-way and failed, a silent word
Awake in some deep pause of waiting worlds,
A murmur suspended in eternity's hush:
But no breath comes from the supernal peace:

A sumptuous interlude occupies the ear
And the heart listens and the soul consents;
An evanescent music it repeats
Wasting on transience Time's eternity. ||53.32||

It was a no-man's-land of evil air,
A crowded neighbourhood without one home,
A borderland between the world and hell. ||56.10||

A formless void suppressed his struggling brain,
A darkness grim and cold oppressed his flesh,
A whispered grey suggestion chilled his heart;
Haled by a serpent-force from its warm home
And dragged to extinction in blank vacancy
Life clung to its seat with cords of gasping breath;
Lapped was his body by a tenebrous tongue. ||60.12||

Each stone was a keen edge of ruthless force
And glued with the chilled blood from tortured breasts;
The dry gnarled trees stood up like dying men
Stiffened into a pose of agony,
And from each window peered an ominous priest
Chanting Te Deums for slaughter's crowning grace,
Cities uprooted, blasted human homes,
Burned writhen bodies, the bombshell's massacre. ||64.13||

It could not house the wideness of a soul
Which needed all infinity for its home. ||66.7||

One sees it circling faithful to its task,
Tireless in an assigned tradition's round;
In decayed and crumbling offices of Time
It keeps close guard in front of custom's wall,
Or in an ancient Night's dim environs
It dozes on a little courtyard's stones
And barks at every unfamiliar light

As at a foe who would break up its home,
A watch-dog of the spirit's sense-railed house
Against intruders from the Invisible,
Nourished on scraps of life and Matter's bones
In its kennel of objective certitude. ||68.12||

There the low bent and mighty figure sits
Bowed under the arc-lamps of her factory-home
Amid the clatter and ringing of her tools. ||68.44||

A power to uplift the laggard world,
Imperious rode a huge high-winged Life-Thought
Unwont to tread the firm unchanging soil:
Accustomed to a blue infinity,
It planed in sunlit sky and starlit air;
It saw afar the unreached Immortal's home
And heard afar the voices of the gods. ||69.2||

But now our rights are barred, our passports void;
We live self-exiled from our heavenlier home. ||40.22||

Our present feels sometimes their regal touch,
Our future strives towards their luminous thrones:
Out of spiritual secrecy they gaze,
Immortal footfalls in mind's corridors sound:
Our souls can climb into the shining planes,
The breadths from which they came can be our home.
Incarnating her beauty in his clasp
She gave for a brief kiss her immortal lips
And drew to her bosom one glorified mortal head:
She made earth her home, for whom heaven was too small. ||72.10||

Its worlds are steps of an ascending Force:
A dream of giant contours, titan lines,
Homes of unfallen and illumined Might,

Heavens of unchanging Good pure and unborn,
Heights of the grandeur of Truth's ageless ray,
As in a symbol sky they start to view
And call our souls into a vaster air. ||73.27||

In each a seraph-winged high-browed Idea
United all knowledge by one master thought,
Persuaded all action to one golden sense,
All powers subjected to a single power
And made a world where it could reign alone,
An absolute ideal's perfect home. ||73.37||

As one drawn to his lost spiritual home
Feels now the closeness of a waiting love,
Into a passage dim and tremulous
That clasped him in from day and night's pursuit,
He travelled led by a mysterious sound. ||75.6||

Into a wonderful bodiless realm he came,
The home of a passion without name or voice,
A depth he felt answering to every height,
A nook was found that could embrace all worlds,
A point that was the conscious knot of space,
An hour eternal in the heart of Time. ||75.15||

Appealing to the soul and not the eye
Beauty lived there at home in her own house,
There all was beautiful by its own right
And needed not the splendour of a robe. ||76.9||

All it became that figures the absolute,
A high vast peak whence spirit could see the worlds,
Calm's wide epiphany, wisdom's mute home,
A lonely station of Omniscience,
A diving-board of the Eternal's power,
A white floor in the house of All-Delight. ||78.7||

All flowed immeasurably to one sea:
All living forms became its atom homes. ||78.30||

All here shall be one day her sweetness's home,
All contraries prepare her harmony;
Towards her our knowledge climbs, our passion gropes,
In her miraculous rapture we shall dwell,
Her clasp will turn to ecstasy our pain. ||81.25||

Armed with the immune occult unsinking Fire
The guardians of Eternity keep its law
For ever fixed upon Truth's giant base
In her magnificent and termless home. ||84.8||

Imagination's great ensorcelling rod
Summoned the unknown and gave to it a home,
Outspread luxuriantly in golden air
Truth's iris-coloured wings of fantasy,
Or sang to the intuitive heart of joy
Wonder's dream-notes that bring the Real close. ||86.13||

There Matter is the Spirit's firm density,
An artistry of glad outwardness of self,
A treasure-house of lasting images
Where sense can build a world of pure delight:
The home of a perpetual happiness,
It lodged the hours as in a pleasant inn. ||86.22||

O Spirit aspiring in an ignorant frame,
O Voice arisen from the Inconscient's world,
How shalt thou speak for men whose hearts are dumb,
Make purblind earth the soul's seer-vision's home
Or lighten the burden of the senseless globe? ||89.14||

Arrived from some half-luminous Beyond
He is a stranger in the mindless vasts;
A traveller in his oft-shifting home
Amid the tread of many infinitudes,
He has pitched a tent of life in desert Space. ||89.25||

Her form retreated from the longing earth
Forsaking nearness to the abandoned sense,
Ascending to her unattainable home. ||92.3||

Arrived upon the strange and dubious globe
The child remembering inly a far home
Lived guarded in her spirit's luminous cell,
Alone mid men in her diviner kind. ||94.19||

Many high gods dwelt in one beautiful home;
Yet was her nature's orb a perfect whole,
Harmonious like a chant with many tones,
Immense and various like a universe. ||94.48||

A land of mountains and wide sun-beat plains
And giant rivers pacing to vast seas,
A field of creation and spiritual hush,
Silence swallowing life's acts into the deeps,
Of thought's transcendent climb and heavenward leap,
A brooding world of reverie and trance,
Filled with the mightiest works of God and man,
Where Nature seemed a dream of the Divine
And beauty and grace and grandeur had their home,
Harboured the childhood of the incarnate Flame. ||95.1||

The great Illusion wraps him in its veils,
The soul's deep intimations come in vain,
In vain is the unending line of seers,
The sages ponder in unsubstantial light,
The poets lend their voice to outward dreams,
A homeless fire inspires the prophet tongues. ||98.24||

But as she moved across the changing earth
A deeper consciousness welled up in her:
A citizen of many scenes and climes,
Each soil and country it has made its home;
It took all clans and peoples for her own,
Till the whole destiny of mankind was hers.
Hamlet and village saw the fate-van pass,
Homes of a life bent to the soil it ploughs
For sustenance of its short and passing days
That, transient, keep their old repeated course
Unchanging in the circle of a sky
Which alters not above our mortal toil. ||99.18||

A few and fit inhabitants she called
To share the glad communion of her peace;
The breadth, the summit were their natural home. ||99.31||

Nameless the austere ascetics without home
Abandoning speech and motion and desire,
Aloof from creatures sat absorbed, alone,
Immaculate in tranquil heights of self
On concentration's luminous voiceless peaks,
World-naked hermits with their matted hair
Immobile as the passionless great hills
Around them grouped like thoughts of some vast mood
Awaiting the Infinite's behest to end. ||99.37||

All she remembered on this day of Fate,
The road that hazarded not the solemn depths
But turned away to flee to human homes,
The wilderness with its mighty monotone,
The morning like a lustrous seer above,
The passion of the summits lost in heaven,
The titan murmur of the endless woods. ||102.1||

I have heard strange voices cross the ether's waves,
The centaur's wizard song has thrilled my ear;
I glimpsed the Apsaras bathing in the pools
And saw the wood-nymphs peering through the leaves;
The winds have shown to me their trampling lords,
I have beheld the princes of the Sun
Burning in thousand-pillared homes of light. ||103.10||

At the path's end through a green cleft in the trees
She saw a clustering line of hermit-routes
And looked now first on her heart's future home,
The thatch that covered the life of Satyavan. ||105.2||

A nave of trees enshrined the hermit thatch,
The new deep covert of her felicity,
Preferred to heaven her soul's temple and home. ||105.9||

Or else it is a wanderer from its home
Who strayed into a blind alley of Time and chance
And finds no issue from a meaningless world. ||107.52||

Although Light grows on earth and Night recedes,
Yet till the evil is slain in its own home
And Light invades the world's inconscient base
And perished has the adversary Force,
He still must labour on, his work half done. ||109.10||

Earth shall be made a home of Heaven's light,
A seer heaven-born shall lodge in human breasts;
The superconscient beam shall touch men's eyes
And the truth-conscious world come down to earth
Invading Matter with the Spirit's ray
Awaking its silence to immortal thoughts,
Awaking the dumb heart to the living Word. ||109.35||

O mortal who complainst of death and fate,
Accuse none of the harms thyself hast called;
This troubled world thou hast chosen for thy home,
Thou art thyself the author of thy pain. ||111.1||

The eternal Consciousness became the home
Of some unsouled almighty Inconscient;
One breathed no more the spirit's native air. ||111.8||

Thus came, born from a blind tremendous choice,
This great perplexed and discontented world,
This haunt of Ignorance, this home of Pain:
There are pitched desire's tents, grief's headquarters. ||111.15||

Away from the strife and suffering on our globe,
He turned towards his far-off blissful home. ||113.2||

Once more she sat behind loud hastening hooves;
A speed of armoured squadrons and a voice
Far-heard of chariots bore her from her home. ||114.7||

In a broad eve with one red eye of cloud,
Through a narrow opening, a green flowered cleft,
Out of the stare of sky and soil they came
Into a mighty home of emerald dusk. ||114.13||

Arrived in that rough-hewn homestead they gave,
Questioning no more the strangeness of her fate,
Their pride and loved one to the great blind king,
A regal pillar of fallen mightiness
And the stately care-worn woman once a queen
Who now hoped nothing for herself from life,
But all things only hoped for her one child,
Calling on that single head from partial Fate
All joy of earth, all heaven's beatitude. ||114.15||

Ours is the home of cosmic certainty. ||120.10||

Outstretching her hands to stay the throng she cried:
"O happy company of luminous gods,
Reveal, who know, the road that I must tread,—
For surely that bright quarter is your home,—
To find the birthplace of the occult Fire
And the deep mansion of my secret soul." ||121.7||

In its deep lotus home her being sat
As if on concentration's marble seat,
Calling the mighty Mother of the worlds
To make this earthly tenement her house. ||127.4||

Out of the infinitudes all came to her,
Into the infinitudes sentient she spread,
Infinity was her own natural home. ||132.22||

Then like a thought fulfilled by some great word
That mightiness assumed a symbol form;
Her being's spaces quivered with its touch,
It covered her as with immortal wings;
On its lips the curve of the unuttered Truth,
A halo of Wisdom's lightnings for its crown,
It entered the mystic lotus in her head,
A thousand-petalled home of power and light. ||134.22||

But Death pealed forth his vast abysmal cry:
"O mortal, turn back to thy transient kind;
Aspire not to accompany Death to his home,
As if thy breath could live where Time must die. ||136.26||

"This is my silent dark immensity,
This is the home of everlasting Night,
This is the secrecy of Nothingness
Entombing the vanity of life's desires. ||137.30||

For only there could dwell the soul's firm truth:
Imperishable, a tongue of sacrifice,
It flamed unquenched upon the central hearth
Where burns for the high house-lord and his mate
The homestead's sentinel and witness fire
From which the altars of the gods are lit. ||142.104||

Think not to plant on earth the living Truth
Or make of Matter's world the home of God;
Truth comes not there but only the thought of Truth,
God is not there but only the name of God. ||144.25||

Truth has no home in earth's irrational breast:
Yet without reason life is a tangle of dreams,
But reason is poised above a dim abyss
And stands at last upon a plank of doubt. ||146.13||

It poured into a navel's lotus depth,
Lodged in the little life-nature's narrow home,
On the body's longings grew heaven-rapture's flower
And made desire a pure celestial flame,
Broke into the cave where coiled World-Energy sleeps
And smote the thousand-hooded serpent Force
That blazing towered and clasped the World-Self above,
Joined Matter's dumbness to the Spirit's hush
And filled earth's acts with the Spirit's silent power. ||147.11||

A marvellous sun looked down from ecstasy's skies
On worlds of deathless bliss, perfection's home,
Magical unfoldings of the Eternal's smile
Capturing his secret heart-beats of delight. ||148.1||

Arisen beneath a triple mystic heaven
The seven immortal earths were seen sublime:
Homes of the blest released from death and sleep

Where grief can never come nor any pang
Arriving from self-lost and seeking worlds
Alter Heaven-nature's changeless quietude
And mighty posture of eternal calm,
Its pose of ecstasy immutable. ||148.10||

Things fashioned were the imaged homes where mind
Arrived to fathom a deep physical joy;
The heart was a torch lit from infinity,
The limbs were trembling densities of soul. ||148.35||

His gaze was the regard of eternity;   OKS
The spirit of its sweet and calm intent
Was a wise home of gladness and divulged
The light of the ages in the mirth of the hours,
A sun of wisdom in a miracled grove. ||149.31||

In the orchestral largeness of his mind
All contrary seekings their close kinship knew,
Rich-hearted, wonderful to each other met
In the mutual marvelling of their myriad notes
And dwelt like brothers of one family
Who had found their common and mysterious home. ||139.32||

Arise, vindicate thy spirit's conquered right:
Relinquishing thy charge of transient breath,
Under the cold gaze of the indifferent stars
Leaving thy borrowed body on the sod,
Ascend, O soul, into thy blissful home. ||150.15||

The heavens were once to me my natural home,
I too have wandered in star-jewelled groves,
Paced sun-gold pastures and moon-silver swards
And heard the harping laughter of their streams
And lingered under branches dropping myrrh;

I too have revelled in the fields of light
Touched by the ethereal raiment of the winds,
Thy wonder-rounds of music I have trod,
Lived in the rhyme of bright unlabouring thoughts,
I have beat swift harmonies of rapture vast,
Danced in spontaneous measures of the soul
The great and easy dances of the gods. ||151.6||

I will fasten thy nature with my cords of strength,
Subdue to my delight thy spirit's limbs
And make thee a vivid knot of all my bliss,
And build in thee my proud and crystal home. ||154.8||

When all thy work in human time is done,
The mind of earth shall be a home of light,
The life of earth a tree growing towards heaven,
The body of earth a tabernacle of God. ||154.11||

It has no home on earth, no centre in man,
Yet is the source of all things thought and done,
The fount of the creation and its works. ||155.26||

All earth shall be the Spirit's manifest home,
Hidden no more by the body and the life,
Hidden no more by the mind's ignorance;
An unerring Hand shall shape event and act. ||155.45||

Awake to his hidden possibility,
Awake to all that slept within his heart
And all that Nature meant when earth was formed
And the Spirit made this ignorant world his home,
He shall aspire to Truth and God and Bliss. ||155.55||

A power leaned down, a happiness found its home. ||156.18||

Outwingings of a bird from its bright home,
Her earthly morns were radiant flights of joy.					||157.12||

Then sighing to her touch the soft-winged sleep
Rose hovering from his flower-like lids and flew
Murmurous away. Awake, he found her eyes
Waiting for his, and felt her hands, and saw
The earth his home given back to him once more
And her made his again, his passion's all.					||157.20||

Look round thee and behold, glad and unchanged
Our home, this forest, with its thousand cries
And the whisper of the wind among the leaves
And, through rifts in emerald scene, the evening sky,
God's canopy of blue sheltering our lives,
And the birds crying for heart's happiness,
Winged poets of our solitary reign,
Our friends on earth where we are king and queen.					||157.25||

Then hand in hand they left that solemn place
Full now of mute unusual memories,
To the green distance of their sylvan home
Returning slowly through the forest's heart:
Round them the afternoon to evening changed;
Light slipped down to the brightly sleeping verge,
And the birds came back winging to their nests,
And day and night leaned to each other's arms.					||157.55||

Murmur and movement and the tread of men
Broke the night's solitude. The neigh of steeds
Rose from the indistinct and voiceful sea
Of life and all along its marchings swelled
The rhyme of hooves, the chariot's homeward voice.					||159.2||

house

The word 'house' appears more than 130 times in this epic of nearly 24,000 lines. Every conceivable use of the word, as noun and verb, in its higher and highest connotations, its mystical overtones, and the magnificence of Sri Aurobindo's poetic language will be found and gradually understood by the 'apt' reader.

There are passages that should be read again and again so that we might take in their mantric force, understanding not with the mind but in the depths of our soul.

Read the passages about the Avatar whom Narad calls 'God's messenger', who comes to earth to uplift humanity and in the most poignant and revelatory lines one can begin to get some understanding of what the Avatar must face and endure. One line that has always moved me deeply speaks to me personally of Sri Aurobindo. "He covers the world's agony with his calm."

There are numerous passages about the house, man's body, that should be read often to become aware of adverse influences that can enter and how we must guard against them.

I remember a friend telling me that he visited Nirodbaran one morning when Arabinda Basu was there for tea time. He mentioned that he was having difficulty understanding Savitri and Arabinda said: "Who told you that you had to understand? Just read it."

Her house of Nature felt an unseen sway,
Illumined swiftly were life's darkened rooms,
And memory's casements opened on the hours
And the tired feet of thought approached her doors. ||2.34||

On the frail breast of this precarious earth,
Since her orbed sight in its breath-fastened house,
Opening in sympathy with happier stars

Where life is not exposed to sorrowful change,
Remembered beauty death-claimed lids ignore
And wondered at this world of fragile forms
Carried on canvas-strips of shimmering Time,
The impunity of unborn Mights was hers. ||4.2||

Out of apprenticeship to Ignorance
Wisdom upraised him to her master craft
And made him an arch-mason of the soul,
A builder of the Immortal's secret house,
An aspirant to supernal Timelessness:
Freedom and empire called to him from on high;
Above mind's twilight and life's star-led night
There gleamed the dawn of a spiritual day. ||5.40||

He owned the house of undivided Time. ||6.17||

There knowledge needs not words to embody Idea;
Idea seeking a house in boundlessness,
Weary of its homeless immortality,
Asks not in thought's carved brilliant cell to rest
Whose single window's clipped outlook on things
Sees only a little arc of God's vast sky. ||6.48||

A voice in the heart uttered the unspoken Name,
A dream of seeking thought wandering through space
Entered the invisible and forbidden house:
The treasure was found of a supernal Day. ||8.27||

When darkness deepens strangling the earth's breast
And man's corporeal mind is the only lamp,
As a thief's in the night shall be the covert tread
Of one who steps unseen into his house. ||11.45||

Even in his mortal session in body's house
An aimless traveller between birth and death,
Ephemeral dreaming of immortality,
To reign she spurs him. He takes up her powers;
He has harnessed her to the yoke of her own law. ||14.14||

The Immanent lives in man as in his house;
He has made the universe his pastime's field,
A vast gymnasium of his works of might. ||15.2||

Late will he know, opening the mystic script,
Whether to a blank port in the Unseen
He goes, or armed with her fiat, to discover
A new mind and body in the city of God
And enshrine the Immortal in his glory's house
And make the finite one with Infinity. ||17.21||

This was a forefront of God's thousandfold house,
Beginnings of the half-screened Invisible. ||23.6||

Earth by this golden superfluity
Bore thinking man and more than man shall bear;
This higher scheme of being is our cause
And holds the key to our ascending fate;
It calls out of our dense mortality
The conscious spirit nursed in Matter's house. ||26.11||

A miracle of the Absolute was born,
Infinity put on a finite soul,
All ocean lived within a wandering drop,
A time-made body housed the Illimitable. ||26.32||

Even in the littleness of our mortal state,
Even in this prison-house of outer form,
A brilliant passage for the infallible Flame

Is driven through gross walls of nerve and brain,
A Splendour presses or a Power breaks through,
Earth's great dull barrier is removed awhile,
The inconscient seal is lifted from our eyes
And we grow vessels of creative might. ||30.5||

A radiance of a golden artifice,
A masterpiece of inspired device and rule,
Her forms hide what they house and only mime
The unseized miracle of self-born shapes
That live for ever in the Eternal's gaze. ||30.9||

For when he strives for things surpassing earth,
Too rude the workman's tools, too crude his stuff,
And hardly with his heart's blood he achieves
His transient house of the divine Idea,
His figure of a Time-inn for the Unborn. ||30.12||

His soul's peak-climb abandoning in its rear
This brilliant courtyard of the House of Days,
He left that fine material Paradise. ||31.21||

Our human ignorance moves towards the Truth
That Nescience may become omniscient:
Transmuted instincts shape to divine thoughts,
Thoughts house infallible immortal sight
And Nature climbs towards God's identity. ||34.11||

There were realms where Knowledge joined creative Power
In her high home and made her all his own:
The grand Illuminate seized her gleaming limbs
And filled them with the passion of his ray
Till all her body was its transparent house
And all her soul a counterpart of his soul. ||35.24||

A wide unquiet mist of seeking space,
A rayless region swallowed in vague swathes,
That seemed, unnamed, unbodied and unhoused,
A swaddled visionless and formless mind,
Asked for a body to translate its soul. ||39.1||

It knew not the Immortal in its house,
It had no greater deeper cause to live. ||42.30||

In limits only it was powerful;
Acute to capture truth for outward use,
Its knowledge was the body's instrument;
Absorbed in the little works of its prison-house
It turned around the same unchanging points
In the same circle of interest and desire,
But thought itself the master of its jail. ||42.31||

A godhead woke but lay with dreaming limbs;
Her house refused to open its sealed doors. ||44.26||

His knowledge dwells in the house of Ignorance;
His force nears not even once the Omnipotent,
Rare are his visits of heavenly ecstasy. ||46.19||

When most unseen, most mightily she works;
Housed in the atom, buried in the clod
Her quick creative passion cannot cease. ||50.42||

Or Beauty shines on them like a wandering star;
Too far to reach, passionate they follow her light;
In Art and Life they catch the All-Beautiful's ray
And make the world their radiant treasure house:
Even common figures are with marvel robed;
A charm and greatness locked in every hour
Awakes the joy which sleeps in all things made. ||51.25||

In the communion of two meeting minds
Thought looked at thought and had no need of speech;
Emotion clasped emotion in two hearts,
They felt each other's thrill in the flesh and nerves
Or melted each in each and grew immense
As when two houses burn and fire joins fire:
Hate grappled hate and love broke in on love,
Will wrestled with will on mind's invisible ground;
Others' sensations passing through like waves
Left quivering the subtle body's frame,
Their anger rushed galloping in brute attack,
A charge of trampling hooves on shaken soil;
One felt another's grief invade the breast,
Another's joy exulting ran through the blood:
Hearts could draw close through distance, voices near
That spoke upon the shore of alien seas. ||51.32||

Identified in soul-vision and soul-sense,
Entering into her depths as into a house,
All he became that she was or longed to be,
He thought with her thoughts and journeyed with her steps,
Lived with her breath and scanned all with her eyes
That he might learn the secret of her soul. ||52.20||

Unseen, a captive in a house of sound,
The spirit lost in the splendour of a dream
Listens to a thousand-voiced illusion's ode. ||53.20||

Only another labyrinthine house
Of creatures and their doings and events,
A city of the traffic of bound souls,
A market of creation and her wares
Was offered to the labouring mind and heart. ||54.29||

A peril haunted now the common air;
The world grew full of menacing Energies,
And wherever turned for help or hope his eyes,
In field and house, in street and camp and mart,
He met the prowl and stealthy come and go
Of armed disquieting bodied Influences. ||56.4||

In street and house, in councils and in courts
Beings he met who looked like living men
And climbed in speech upon high wings of thought
But harboured all that is subhuman, vile
And lower than the lowest reptile's crawl.
The Anarchs of the formless depths arose,
Great titan beings and demoniac powers,
World-egos racked with lust and thought and will,
Vast minds and lives without a spirit within:
Impatient architects of error's house,
Leaders of the cosmic ignorance and unrest
And sponsors of sorrow and mortality
Embodied the dark Ideas of the Abyss. ||61.5||

He saw in Night the Eternal's shadowy veil,
Knew death for a cellar of the house of life,
In destruction felt creation's hasty pace,
Knew loss as the price of a celestial gain
And hell as a short cut to heaven's gates. ||64.38||

Then in Illusion's occult factory
And in the Inconscient's magic printing house
Torn were the formats of the primal Night
And shattered the stereotypes of Ignorance. ||64.49||

It could not house the wideness of a soul
Which needed all infinity for its home. ||66.60||

Advancing tardily from a limping start,
Crutching hypothesis upon argument,
Throning its theories as certitudes,
It reasons from the half-known to the unknown,
Ever constructing its frail house of thought,
Ever undoing the web that it has spun. ||66.17||

One sees it circling faithful to its task,
Tireless in an assigned tradition's round;
In decayed and crumbling offices of Time
It keeps close guard in front of custom's wall,
Or in an ancient Night's dim environs
It dozes on a little courtyard's stones
And barks at every unfamiliar light
As at a foe who would break up its home,
A watch-dog of the spirit's sense-railed house
Against intruders from the Invisible,
Nourished on scraps of life and Matter's bones
In its kennel of objective certitude. ||68.12||

Arriving late from a far plane of thought
Into a packed irrational world of Chance
Where all was grossly felt and blindly done,
Yet the haphazard seemed the inevitable,
Came Reason, the squat godhead artisan,
To her narrow house upon a ridge in Time. ||68.36||

At will she spaces in thin air of mind
Like maps in the school-house of intellect hung,
Forcing wide Truth into a narrow scheme,
Her numberless warring strict philosophies;
Out of Nature's body of phenomenon
She carves with Thought's keen edge in rigid lines
Like rails for the World-Magician's power to run,
Her sciences precise and absolute. ||68.47||

Arch-masons of the eternal Thaumaturge,
Moulders and measurers of fragmented space,
They have made their plan of the concealed and known
A dwelling-house for the invisible King. ||71.11||

This was the play of the bright gods of Thought.
Attracting into time the timeless Light,
Imprisoning eternity in the hours,
This they have planned, to snare the feet of Truth
In an aureate net of concept and of phrase
And keep her captive for the thinker's joy
In his little world built of immortal dreams:
There must she dwell mured in the human mind,
An empress prisoner in her subject's house,
Adored and pure and still on his heart's throne,
His splendid property cherished and apart
In the wall of silence of his secret muse,
Immaculate in white virginity,
The same for ever and for ever one,
His worshipped changeless Goddess through all time. ||75.2||

In our thinking's close and narrow lamp-lit house
The vanity of our shut mortal mind
Dreams that the chains of thought have made her ours;
But only we play with our own brilliant bonds;
Tying her down, it is ourselves we tie. ||72.16||

At each pace of the journey marvellous
A new degree of wonder and of bliss,
A new rung formed in Being's mighty stair,
A great wide step trembling with jewelled fire
As if a burning spirit quivered there
Upholding with his flame the immortal hope,
As if a radiant God had given his soul
That he might feel the tread of pilgrim feet
Mounting in haste to the Eternal's house. ||73.55||

There is the secrecy of the House of Flame,
The blaze of Godlike thought and golden bliss,
The rapt idealism of heavenly sense;
There are the wonderful voices, the sun-laugh,
A gurgling eddy in rivers of God's joy,
And the mysteried vineyards of the gold moon-wine,
All the fire and sweetness of which hardly here
A brilliant shadow visits mortal life. ||73.18||

In a veiled Nature's hallowed secrecies
It burns for ever on the altar Mind,
Its priests the souls of dedicated gods,
Humanity its house of sacrifice. ||73.24||

A frail house hanging in uncertain air,
The thin ingenious web round which it moves,
Put out awhile on the tree of the universe,
And gathered up into itself again,
Was only a trap to catch life's insect food,
Winged thoughts that flutter fragile in brief light
But dead, once captured in fixed forms of mind,
Aims puny but looming large in man's small scale,
Flickers, of imagination's brilliant gauze
And cobweb-wrapped beliefs alive no more. ||74.21||

Our mind is a house haunted by the slain past,
Ideas soon mummified, ghosts of old truths,
God's spontaneities tied with formal strings
And packed into drawers of reason's trim bureau,
A grave of great lost opportunities,
Or an office for misuse of soul and life
And all the waste man makes of heaven's gifts
And all his squanderings of Nature's store,
A stage for the comedy of Ignorance. ||74.24||

Appealing to the soul and not the eye
Beauty lived there at home in her own house,
There all was beautiful by its own right
And needed not the splendour of a robe. ||76.9||

All it became that figures the absolute,
A high vast peak whence spirit could see the worlds,
Calm's wide epiphany, wisdom's mute home,
A lonely station of Omniscience,
A diving-board of the Eternal's power,
A white floor in the house of All-Delight. ||78.7||

All he had done was to prepare a field;
His small beginnings asked for a mighty end:
For all that he had been must now new-shape
In him her joy to embody, to enshrine
Her beauty and greatness in his house of life. ||82.4||

Attuning to one Truth their own right rule
Each housed the gladness of a bright degree,
Alone in beauty, perfect in self-kind,
An image cast by one deep truth's absolute,
Married to all in happy difference. ||86.2||

A vast Truth-Consciousness took up these signs
To pass them on to some divine child Heart
That looked on them with laughter and delight
And joyed in these transcendent images
Living and real as the truths they house. ||86.7||

The Spirit's white neutrality became
A playground of miracles, a rendezvous
For the secret powers of a mystic Timelessness:
It made of space a marvel house of God,
It poured through Time its works of ageless might,

Unveiled seen as a luring rapturous face
The wonder and beauty of its Love and Force. ||86.8||

The eternal Goddess moved in her cosmic house
Sporting with God as a Mother with her child:
To him the universe was her bosom of love,
His toys were the immortal verities. ||86.9||

There Matter is the Spirit's firm density,
An artistry of glad outwardness of self,
A treasure-house of lasting images
Where sense can build a world of pure delight:
The home of a perpetual happiness,
It lodged the hours as in a pleasant inn. ||86.22||

An architect hewing out self's living rock,
Phenomenon built Reality's summer-house
On the beaches of the sea of Infinity. ||86.29||

Heaven's fixed regard beholds him from above,
In the house of Nature a perturbing guest,
A voyager twixt Thought's inconstant shores,
A hunter of unknown and beautiful Powers,
A nomad of the far mysterious Light,
In the wide ways a little spark of God. ||89.26||

A witness to God's parley with the Night
It leaned compassionate from immortal calm
And housed desire, the troubled seed of things. ||89.61||

Across the light of fast-receding planes
That fled from him as from a falling star
Compelled to fill his human house in Time
His soul drew back into the speed and noise
Of the vast business of created things. ||92.8||

A world translated was her gleaming mind,
And marvel-mooned bright crowding fantasies
Fed with spiritual sustenance of dreams
The ideal goddess in her house of gold. ||94.32||

Overcoming invisible hedge and masked defence
And the loneliness that separates soul from soul,
She wished to make all one immense embrace
That she might house in it all living things
Raised into a splendid point of seeing light
Out of division's dense inconscient cleft,
And make them one with God and world and her. ||95.18||

Angrily enamoured of her sweet passionate ray
The weakness of their earth could hardly bear,
They longed but cried out at the touch desired
Inapt to meet divinity so close,
Intolerant of a Force they could not house. ||95.38||

A single lamp lit in perfection's house,
A bright pure image in a priestless shrine,
Alone amid surrounding crowds she dwelt,
Apart in herself until her hour of fate. ||97.13||

Authors of earth's high change, to you it is given
To cross the dangerous spaces of the soul
And touch the mighty Mother stark awake
And meet the Omnipotent in this house of flesh
And make of life the million-bodied One. ||98.14||

Here were disclosed to her the mystic courts,
The lurking doors of beauty and surprise,
The wings that murmur in the golden house,
The temple of sweetness and the fiery aisle. ||101.21||

As might a soul on Nature's background limned
Stand out for a moment in a house of dream
Created by the ardent breath of life,
So he appeared against the forest verge
Inset twixt green relief and golden ray. ||102.8||

At first her glance that took life's million shapes
Impartially to people its treasure-house
Along with sky and flower and hill and star,
Dwelt rather on the bright harmonious scene. ||102.19||

Awake to Nature, vague as yet to life,
The eager prisoner from the Infinite,
The immortal wrestler in its mortal house,
Its pride, power, passion of a striving God,
It saw this image of veiled deity,
This thinking master creature of the earth,
This last result of the beauty of the stars,
But only saw like fair and common forms
The artist spirit needs not for its work
And puts aside in memory's shadowy rooms. ||102.21||

In the great tapestried chambers of her state
Free in her boundless palace I have dwelt
Indulged by the warm mother of us all,
Reared with my natural brothers in her house
I lay in the wide bare embrace of heaven,
The sunlight's radiant blessing clasped my brow,
The moonbeam's silver ecstasy at night
Kissed my dim lids to sleep. Earth's morns were mine;
Lured by faint murmurings with the green-robed hours
I wandered lost in woods, prone to the voice
Of winds and waters, partner of the sun's joy,
A listener to the universal speech:
My spirit satisfied within me knew
Godlike our birthright, luxuried our life
Whose close belongings are the earth and skies. ||103.29||

In men I met strange portions of a Self
That sought for fragments and in fragments lived:
Each lived in himself and for himself alone
And with the rest joined only fleeting ties;
Each passioned over his surface joy and grief,
Nor saw the Eternal in his secret house. ||103.40||

But I must haste back to my father's house
Which soon will lose one loved accustomed tread
And listen in vain for a once cherished voice. ||105.6||

O thou who hast come to this great perilous world
Now only seen through the splendour of thy dreams,
Where hardly love and beauty can live safe,
Thyself a being dangerously great,
A soul alone in a golden house of thought
Has lived walled in by the safety of thy dreams. ||106.38||

Along the dreadful causeway of the gods
Armoured with love and faith and sacred joy,
A traveller to the Eternal's house
Once let unwounded pass a mortal life." ||106.61||

Or if crouches unseen a panther doom,
If wings of Evil brood above that house,
Then also speak, that we may turn aside
And rescue our lives from hazard of wayside doom
And chance entanglement of an alien fate." ||106.98||

A grisly company of maladies
Come, licensed lodgers, into man's bodily house,
Purveyors of death and torturers of life. ||107.20||

Even worse may be the cost, direr the pain:
His large identity and all-harbouring love
Shall bring the cosmic anguish into his depths,
The sorrow of all living things shall come
And knock at his doors and live within his house;
A dreadful cord of sympathy can tie
All suffering into his single grief and make
All agony in all the worlds his own. ||108.48||

This mortal life shall house Eternity's bliss,
The body's self taste immortality. ||109.36||

A Mind arose that stared at Nothingness
Till figures formed of what could never be;
It housed the contrary of all that is. ||111.6||

Conquer thy heart's throbs, let thy heart beat in God:
Thy nature shall be the engine of his works,
Thy voice shall house the mightiness of his Word:
Then shalt thou harbour my force and conquer Death." ||116.26||

In the indeterminate formlessness of Self
Creation took its first mysterious steps,
It made the body's shape a house of soul
And Matter learned to think and person grew;
She saw Space peopled with the seeds of life
And saw the human creature born in Time. ||117.2||

Mind nascent laboured out a mutable form,
It built a mobile house on shifting sands,
A floating isle upon a bottomless sea. ||117.7||

It felt a godhead in its fragile house;
It saw blue heavens, dreamed immortality. ||117.9||

A conscious soul in the Inconscient's world
Hidden behind our thoughts and hopes and dreams,
An indifferent Master signing Nature's acts
Leaves the vicegerent mind a seeming king.
In his floating house upon the sea of Time
This regent sits at work and never rests:
He is a puppet of the dance of Time;
He is driven by the hours, the moment's call
Compels him with the thronging of life's need
And the babel of the voices of the world. ||117.11||

I have included the four lines from the preceding passage for a more
complete understanding.

*In the passage above Sri Aurobindo tells us that there is a conscious
soul who is hidden behind our thoughts, etc. and this 'Master' leaves the
vicegerent mind in control, but this 'mind' is actually a puppet and is
driven by many impulses and voices, the hours, the moment's call, life's
needs and in an extraordinary line,*

"And the babel of the voices of the world".

Note that this is not a babble as occurs in another passage in Savitri, but
a reference to Babel, an ancient city in Shinar where the building of a
tower to reach heaven was attempted but failed because of the inability
of a thousand different unintelligible voices to understand each other.

Man's house of life holds not the gods alone:
There are occult Shadows, there are tenebrous Powers,
Inhabitants of life's ominous nether rooms,
A shadowy world's stupendous denizens. ||117.24||

A careless guardian of his nature's powers,
Man harbours dangerous forces in his house. ||117.25||

The dreadful powers held down within his depths
Become his masters or his ministers;
Enormous they invade his bodily house,
Can act in his acts, infest his thought and life. ||117.28||

Impotent to quell his terrible prisoners
Appalled the householder helpless sits above,
Taken from him his house is his no more. ||117.33||

In house and house the huge uprising grows;
Hell's companies are loosed to do their work,
Into the earth-ways they break out from all doors,
Invade with blood-lust and the will to slay
And fill with horror and carnage God's fair world. ||117.41||

This evil Nature housed in human hearts
A foreign inhabitant, a dangerous guest:
The soul that harbours it it can dislodge,
Expel the householder, possess the house. ||117.43||

All the world's possibilities in man
Are waiting as the tree waits in its seed:
His past lives in him; it drives his future's pace;
His present's acts fashion his coming fate.
The unborn gods hide in his house of Life. ||117.49||

Although the last line in which we find the word 'house' is a full sentence, I have included the four previous lines to give us the full power of the passage. Those who have tended the earth, grown trees and flowers, developed an intimacy and harmony with Nature will respond with a quiet joy to the first two lines which take us even beyond Nature to man's possibilities.

Our inner Mind dwells in a larger light,
Its brightness looks at us through hidden doors;

Our members luminous grow and Wisdom's face
Appears in the doorway of the mystic ward:
When she enters into our house of outward sense,
Then we look up and see, above, her sun. ||117.78||

He saw his being's unrealised vastnesses,
He aspired and housed the nascent demi-god. ||117.83||

Thus man in his little house made of earth's dust
Grew towards an unseen heaven of thought and dream
Looking into the vast vistas of his mind
On a small globe dotting infinity. ||117.85||

What transcendent beauty and vision we find in these four lines.   Once
there was a photo in a local newspaper in Pondicherry taken by one of
the astronauts and it clearly showed a bright white light directly over
the city.

But when she came back to her self of thought,
Once more she was a human thing on earth,
A lump of Matter, a house of closed sight,
A mind compelled to think out ignorance,
A life-force pressed into a camp of works
And the material world her limiting field. ||118.3||

A royalty without freedom was her lot;
The sovereign throned obeyed her ministers:
Her servants mind and sense governed her house
And guarded with a phalanx of armoured rules
The reason's balanced reign, kept order and peace. ||119.5||

Or else for the body of some high Idea
A house was built with too close-fitting bricks;
Action and thought cemented made a wall
Of small ideals limiting the soul. ||119.16||

"Who then is this who knows not that the soul
Is a least gland or a secretion's fault
Disquieting the sane government of the mind,
Disordering the function of the brain,
Or a yearning lodged in Nature's mortal house
Or dream whispered in man's cave of hollow thought
Who would prolong his brief unhappy term
Or cling to living in a sea of death?" ||120.26||

I am woman, nurse and slave and beaten beast;
I tend the hands that gave me cruel blows;
The hearts that spurned my love and zeal I serve;
I am the courted queen, the pampered doll,
I am the giver of the bowl of rice,
I am the worshipped Angel of the House. ||122.9||

Although I live in Time besieged by Death,
Precarious owner of my body and soul
Housed on a little speck amid the stars,
For me and my use the universe was made. ||123.35||

I have tamed the wild beast trained to be my friend;
He guards my house, looks up waiting my will. ||123.49||

In their immensitude signing infinity
They were the extension of the self of God
And housed, impassively receiving all,
His figures and his small and mighty acts
And his passion and his birth and life and death
And his return to immortality. ||125.28||

A house was there all made of flame and light
And crossing a wall of doorless living fire
There suddenly she met her secret soul. ||125.39||

In its deep lotus home her being sat
As if on concentration's marble seat,
Calling the mighty Mother of the worlds
To make this earthly tenement her house. ||127.4||

Impenetrable, withheld from mortal sense,
The inner chambers of the spirit's house
Disclosed to her their happenings and their guests;
Eyes looked through crevices in the invisible wall
And through the secrecy of the unseen doors
There came into mind's little frontal room
Thoughts that enlarged our limited human range,
Lifted the ideal's half-quenched or sinking torch
Or peered through the finite at the infinite. ||129.18||

So man evolving to divinest heights
Colloques still with the animal and the Djinn;
The human godhead with star-gazer eyes
Lives still in one house with the primal beast. ||129.25||

If that retired, all objects would be extinct,
Her private universe would cease to be,
The house she had built with bricks of thought and sense
In the beginning after the birth of Space. ||130.13||

In this black dream which was a house of Void,
A walk to Nowhere in a land of Nought,
Ever they drifted without aim or goal;
Gloom led to worse gloom, death to an emptier death,
In some positive Non-Being's purposeless Vast
Through formless wastes dumb and unknowable. ||138.2||

Here in this seat of Darkness mute and lone,
In the heart of everlasting Nothingness
Light conquered now even by that feeble beam:

Its faint infiltration drilled the blind deaf mass;
Almost it changed into a glimmering sight
That housed the phantom of an aureate Sun
Whose orb pupilled the eye of Nothingness. ||138.16||

This angel in thy body thou callst love,
Who shapes his wings from thy emotion's hues,
In a ferment of thy body has been born
And with the body that housed it it must die. ||140.2||

O traveller in the chariot of the Sun,
High priestess in the holy fancy's shrine
Who with a magic ritual in earth's house
Worshippest ideal and eternal love,
What is this love thy thought has deified,
This sacred legend and immortal myth? ||140.28||

All thy high dreams were made by Matter's mind
To solace its dull work in Matter's jail,
Its only house where it alone seems true. ||140.82||

In waking Mind, the Thinker built his house. ||141.15||

A mute Delight regards Time's countless works:
To house God's joy in things Space gave wide room,
To house God's joy in self our souls were born. ||142.14||

This universe an old enchantment guards;
Its objects are carved cups of World-Delight
Whose charmed wine is some deep soul's rapture-drink:
The All-Wonderful has packed heaven with his dreams,
He has made blank ancient Space his marvel-house;
He spilled his spirit into Matter's signs:
His fires of grandeur burn in the great sun,
He glides through heaven shimmering in the moon;

He is beauty carolling in the fields of sound;
He chants the stanzas of the odes of Wind;
He is silence watching in the stars at night;
He wakes at dawn and calls from every bough,
Lies stunned in the stone and dreams in flower and tree. ||142.5||

Death from the incredulous Darkness sent its cry:
"O priestess in Imagination's house,
Persuade first Nature's fixed immutable laws
And make the impossible thy daily work. ||142.44||

And thou shalt harvest in thy joyful house
Felicity of thy surrounded eves. ||142.72||

But now her spirit's flame of conscient force
Retiring from a sweetness without fruit
Called back her thoughts from speech to sit within
In a deep room in meditation's house. ||142.103||

For only there could dwell the soul's firm truth:
Imperishable, a tongue of sacrifice,
It flamed unquenched upon the central hearth
Where burns for the high house-lord and his mate
The homestead's sentinel and witness fire
From which the altars of the gods are lit. ||142.104||

There is no house for him in hurrying Time. ||144.11||

Look on these forms that stay awhile and pass,
These lives that long and strive, then are no more,
These structures that have no abiding truth,
The saviour creeds that cannot save themselves,
But perish in the strangling hands of the years,
Discarded from man's thought, proved false by Time,
Philosophies that strip all problems bare

But nothing ever have solved since earth began,
And sciences omnipotent in vain
By which men learn of what the suns are made,
Transform all forms to serve their outward needs,
Ride through the sky and sail beneath the sea,
But learn not what they are or why they came;
These polities, architectures of man's brain,
That, bricked with evil and good, wall in man's spirit
And, fissured houses, palace at once and jail,
Rot while they reign and crumble before they crash;
These revolutions, demon or drunken god,
Convulsing the wounded body of mankind
Only to paint in new colours an old face;
These wars, carnage triumphant, ruin gone mad,
The work of centuries vanishing in an hour,
The blood of the vanquished and the victor's crown
Which men to be born must pay for with their pain,
The hero's face divine on satyr's limbs,
The demon's grandeur mixed with the demi-god's,
The glory and the beasthood and the shame;
Why is it all, the labour and the din,
The transient joys, the timeless sea of tears,
The longing and the hoping and the cry,
The battle and the victory and the fall,
The aimless journey that can never pause,
The waking toil, the incoherent sleep? ||144.14||

But how shall I seek rest in endless peace
Who house the mighty Mother's violent force,
Her vision turned to read the enigmaed world,
Her will tempered in the blaze of Wisdom's sun
And the flaming silence of her heart of love? ||144.39||

My mind is a torch lit from the eternal sun,
My life a breath drawn by the immortal Guest,
My mortal body is the Eternal's house. ||144.45||

Already the torch becomes the undying ray,
Already the life is the Immortal's force,
The house grows of the householder part and one. ||144.46||

I am not bound by thought or sense or shape;
I live in the glory of the Infinite,
I am near to the Nameless and Unknowable,
The Ineffable is now my household mate. ||144.51||

But the soul grows concealed within its house;
It gives to the body its strength and magnificence;
It follows aims in an ignorant aimless world,
It lends significance to earth's meaningless life. ||146.42||

On summit Mind are radiant altitudes
Exposed to the lustre of Infinity,
Outskirts and dependences of the house of Truth,
Upraised estates of Mind and measureless. ||146.48||

Then stretches the boundless finite's last expanse,
The cosmic empire of the Overmind,
Time's buffer state bordering Eternity,
Too vast for the experience of man's soul:
All here gathers beneath one golden sky:
The Powers that build the cosmos station take
In its house of infinite possibility;
Each god from there builds his own nature's world;
Ideas are phalanxed like a group of sums;
Thought crowds in masses seized by one regard;
All Time is one body, Space a single book:
There is the Godhead's universal gaze
And there the boundaries of immortal Mind:
The line that parts and joins the hemispheres
Closes in on the labour of the Gods
Fencing eternity from the toil of Time. ||146.54||

In her glorious kingdom of eternal light
All-ruler, ruled by none, the Truth supreme,
Omnipotent, omniscient and alone,
In a golden country keeps her measureless house;
In its corridor she hears the tread that comes
Out of the Unmanifest never to return
Till the Unknown is known and seen by men. ||146.55||

A halo of the indwelling Deity,
The Immortal's lustre that had lit her face
And tented its radiance in her body's house,
Overflowing made the air a luminous sea. ||147.4||

A little figure in infinity
Yet stood and seemed the Eternal's very house,
As if the world's centre was her very soul
And all wide space was but its outer robe. ||147.6||

Relieve the radiant god from thy black mask;
Release the soul of the world called Satyavan
Freed from thy clutch of pain and ignorance
That he may stand master of life and fate,
Man's representative in the house of God,
The mate of Wisdom and the spouse of Light,
The eternal bridegroom of the eternal bride." ||147.24||

Firm in the bosom of immensity
Spiritual breadths were seen, sublimely born
From a still beauty of creative joy;
Embodied thoughts to sweet dimensions held
To please some carelessness of divine peace,
Answered the deep demand of an infinite sense
And its need of forms to house its bodiless thrill. ||148.8||

O Sun-Word, thou shalt raise the earth-soul to Light
And bring down God into the lives of men;
Earth shall be my work-chamber and my house,
My garden of life to plant a seed divine. ||154.10||

Mind is not all his tireless climb can reach,
There is a fire on the apex of the worlds,
There is a house of the Eternal's Light. ||155.15||

A soul shall wake in the Inconscient's house;
The mind shall be God-vision's tabernacle,
The body intuition's instrument,
And life a channel for God's visible power. ||155.44||

This world shall be God's visible garden-house,
The earth shall be a field and camp of God,
Man shall forget consent to mortality
And his embodied frail impermanence. ||155.47||

For it is given back, but it is known,
A playing ground and dwelling house of God
Who hides himself in bird and beast and man
Sweetly to find himself again by love,
By oneness. His presence leads the rhythms of life
That seek for mutual joy in spite of pain. ||157.45||

Behold, at noon leaving this house of clay
I wandered in far-off eternities,
Yet still, a captive in her golden hands,
I tread your little hillock called green earth
And in the moments of your transient sun
Live glad among the busy works of men." ||158.18||

monuments

A breath comes down from a supernal air,
A presence is borne, a guiding Light awakes,
A stillness falls upon the instruments:
Fixed sometimes like a marble monument,
Stone-calm, the body is a pedestal
Supporting a figure of eternal Peace. ||10.14||

A marble monument of ponderings, shone
A forehead, sight's crypt, and large like ocean's gaze
Towards Heaven two tranquil eyes of boundless thought
Looked into man's and saw the god to come. ||89.11||

His shape was nothingness made real, his limbs
Were monuments of transience and beneath
Brows of unwearying calm large godlike lids
Silent beheld the writhing serpent, life. ||135.11||

Enigma of the Inconscient's sculptural sleep,
Symbols of the approach to darkness old
And monuments of her titanic reign,
Opening to depths like dumb appalling jaws
That wait a traveller down a haunted path
Attracted to a mystery that slays,
They watched across her road, cruel and still;
Sentinels they stood of dumb Necessity,
Mute heads of vigilant and sullen gloom,
Carved muzzle of a dim enormous world. ||136.24||

nave

A nave of trees enshrined the hermit thatch,
The new deep covert of her felicity,
Preferred to heaven her soul's temple and home. ||105.9||

palace

Around him crowded grey and squalid huts
Neighbouring proud palaces of perverted Power,
Inhuman quarters and demoniac wards. ||58.5||

When the pale dawn slipped through Night's shadowy guard,
Vainly the new-born light desired her face;
The palace woke to its own emptiness;
The sovereign of its daily joys was far;
Her moonbeam feet tinged not the lucent floors:
The beauty and divinity were gone. ||98.63||

Often from gilded dusk to argent dawn
Where jewel-lamps flickered on frescoed walls
And the stone lattice stared at moonlit boughs,
Half-conscious of the tardy listening night
Dimly she glided between banks of sleep
At rest in the slumbering palaces of kings. ||99.17||

In the great tapestried chambers of her state
Free in her boundless palace I have dwelt
Indulged by the warm mother of us all,
Reared with my natural brothers in her house
I lay in the wide bare embrace of heaven,
The sunlight's radiant blessing clasped my brow,
The moonbeam's silver ecstasy at night
Kissed my dim lids to sleep. Earth's morns were mine;
Lured by faint murmurings with the green-robed hours
I wandered lost in woods, prone to the voice
Of winds and waters, partner of the sun's joy,
A listener to the universal speech:
My spirit satisfied within me knew
Godlike our birthright, luxuried our life
Whose close belongings are the earth and skies. ||103.29||

As might a lightning streak, a glory fell
Nearing until the rapt eyes of the sage
Looked out from luminous cloud and, strangely limned
His face, a beautiful mask of antique joy,
Appearing in light descended where arose
King Aswapathy's palace to the winds
In Madra, flowering up in delicate stone. ||106.14||

Here is no cause for dread, no chance for grief
To raise her ominous head and stare at love:
A single spirit in a multitude,
Happy is Satyavan mid earthly men
Whom Savitri has chosen for her mate,
And fortunate the forest hermitage
Where leaving her palace and riches and a throne
My Savitri will dwell and bring in heaven. ||106.94||

At first to her beneath the sapphire heavens
The sylvan solitude was a gorgeous dream,
An altar of the summer's splendour and fire,
A sky-topped flower-hung palace of the gods
And all its scenes a smile on rapture's lips
And all its voices bards of happiness. ||115.1||

Our body's subtle self is throned within
In its viewless palace of veridical dreams
That are bright shadows of the thoughts of God. ||117.80||

Look on these forms that stay awhile and pass,
These lives that long and strive, then are no more,
These structures that have no abiding truth,
The saviour creeds that cannot save themselves,
But perish in the strangling hands of the years,
Discarded from man's thought, proved false by Time,

Philosophies that strip all problems bare
But nothing ever have solved since earth began,
And sciences omnipotent in vain
By which men learn of what the suns are made,
Transform all forms to serve their outward needs,
Ride through the sky and sail beneath the sea,
But learn not what they are or why they came;
These polities, architectures of man's brain,
That, bricked with evil and good, wall in man's spirit
And, fissured houses, palace at once and jail,
Rot while they reign and crumble before they crash;
These revolutions, demon or drunken god,
Convulsing the wounded body of mankind
Only to paint in new colours an old face;
These wars, carnage triumphant, ruin gone mad,
The work of centuries vanishing in an hour,
The blood of the vanquished and the victor's crown
Which men to be born must pay for with their pain,
The hero's face divine on satyr's limbs,
The demon's grandeur mixed with the demi-god's,
The glory and the beasthood and the shame;
Why is it all, the labour and the din,
The transient joys, the timeless sea of tears,
The longing and the hoping and the cry,
The battle and the victory and the fall,
The aimless journey that can never pause,
The waking toil, the incoherent sleep? ||144.14||

shrine

In these passages in which we find the word 'shrine' we see it used
as a verb as well as a noun and the four lines where Sri Aurobindo
describes a magic hut of certitude in which its image of the Real is
shrined collapses into the Nescience. We even find the words enshrine in
a passage of five lines in Book II, Canto II, The Adoration of the Divine
Mother and the past tense, enshrined in Book VII, Canto I. We must
aspire to read Savitri more slowly with the understanding that every

word has significance and even an 'and' or a 'the' has been consciously chosen by Sri Aurobindo as the inevitable word required.

Well might he find in her his perfect shrine. ||3.28||

Late will he know, opening the mystic script,
Whether to a blank port in the Unseen
He goes, or armed with her fiat, to discover
A new mind and body in the city of God
And enshrine the Immortal in his glory's house
And make the finite one with Infinity. ||17.21||

Impassive he lived immune from earthly hopes,
A figure in the ineffable Witness' shrine
Pacing the vast cathedral of his thoughts
Under its arches dim with infinity
And heavenward brooding of invisible wings. ||20.4||

An Omniscient knowing without sight or thought,
An indecipherable Omnipotence,
A mystic Form that could contain the worlds,
Yet make one human breast its passionate shrine,
Drew him out of his seeking loneliness
Into the magnitudes of God's embrace. ||21.4||

All worlds she makes the partners of her deeds,
Accomplices of her mighty violence,
Her daring leaps into the impossible:
From every source she has taken her cunning means,
She draws from the free-love marriage of the planes
Elements for her creation's tour-de-force:
A wonder-weft of knowledge incalculable,
A compendium of divine invention's feats
She has combined to make the unreal true
Or liberate suppressed reality:

In her unhedged Circean wonderland
Pell-mell she shepherds her occult mightinesses;
Her mnemonics of the craft of the Infinite,
Jets of the screened subliminal's caprice,
Tags of the gramarye of Inconscience,
Freedom of a sovereign Truth without a law,
Thoughts that were born in the immortals' world,
Oracles that break out from behind the shrine,
Warnings from the daemonic inner voice
And peeps and lightning-leaps of prophecy
And intimations to the inner ear,
Abrupt interventions stark and absolute
And the superconscient's unaccountable acts,
Have woven her balanced web of miracles
And the weird technique of her tremendous art. ||22.20||

Pity is there and fire-winged sacrifice,
And flashes of sympathy and tenderness
Cast heaven-lights from the heart's secluded shrine.
None truly knew himself or knew the world
Or the Reality living there enshrined:
Only they knew what Mind could take and build
Out of the secret Supermind's huge store. ||51.40||

A shadow fell across the simple Ray:
Obscured was the Truth-light in the cavern heart
That burns unwitnessed in the altar crypt
Behind the still velamen's secrecy
Companioning the Godhead of the shrine. ||62.13||

Always the dark Adventurers seem to win;
Nature they fill with evil's institutes,
Turn into defeats the victories of Truth,
Proclaim as falsehoods the eternal laws,
And load the dice of Doom with wizard lies;
The world's shrines they have occupied, usurped its thrones. ||63.6||

The magic hut of built-up certitudes
Made out of glittering dust and bright moonshine
In which it shrines its image of the Real,
Collapsed into the Nescience whence it rose. ||74.22||

All he had done was to prepare a field;
His small beginnings asked for a mighty end:
For all that he had been must now new-shape
In him her joy to embody, to enshrine
Her beauty and greatness in his house of life. ||82.4||

Its Power that makes the unknowable near and true,
In the temple of the ideal shrined the One:
It peopled thought and mind and happy sense
Filled with bright aspects of the might of God
And living persons of the one Supreme,
The speech that voices the ineffable,
The ray revealing unseen Presences,
The virgin forms through which the Formless shines,
The Word that ushers divine experience
And the Ideas that crowd the Infinite. ||86.14||

Upward it rose to grasp the human scene:
The strong Inhabitant turned to watch her field,
A lovelier light assumed her spirit brow
And sweet and solemn grew her musing gaze;
Celestial-human deep warm slumbrous fires
Woke in the long fringed glory of her eyes
Like altar-burnings in a mysteried shrine. ||94.42||

A single lamp lit in perfection's house,
A bright pure image in a priestless shrine,
Alone amid surrounding crowds she dwelt,
Apart in herself until her hour of fate. ||97.13||

He has lost the inner Voice that led his thoughts,
And masking the oracular tripod seat
A specious Idol fills the marvel shrine. ||98.23||

Advancing amid tall heaven-pillaring trees,
Apparelled in her flickering-coloured robe,
She seemed burning towards the eternal realms
A bright moved torch of incense and of flame
That from the sky-roofed temple-soil of earth
A pilgrim hand lifts in an invisible shrine. ||98.30||

Escaped from surface sight and mortal sense
The seizing harmony of its shapes became
The strange significant icon of a Power
Renewing its inscrutable descent
Into a human figure of its works
That stood out in life's bold abrupt relief
On the soil of the evolving universe,
A godhead sculptured on a wall of thought,
Mirrored in the flowing hours and dimly shrined
In Matter as in a cathedral cave. ||98.37||

O my bright beauty's princess, Savitri,
By my delight and thy own joy compelled
Enter my life, thy chamber and thy shrine. ||103.75||

A nave of trees enshrined the hermit thatch,
The new deep covert of her felicity,
Preferred to heaven her soul's temple and home. ||105.9||

The rich and happy secrecy that once
Enshrined her as if in a silver bower
Apart in a bright nest of thoughts and dreams
Made room for tragic hours of solitude
And lonely grief that none could share or know,
A body seeing the end too soon of joy
And the fragile happiness of its mortal love. ||115.17||

Moved by the Presences with which he yearns,
He offers in implacable shrines his soul
And clothes all with the beauty of his dreams. ||137.42||

Blind slave of my deaf force whom I compel
To sin that I may punish, to desire
That I may scourge thee with despair and grief
And thou come bleeding to me at the last,
Thy nothingness recognised, my greatness known,
Turn nor attempt forbidden happy fields
Meant for the souls that can obey my law,
Lest in their sombre shrines thy tread awake
From their uneasy iron-hearted sleep
The Furies who avenge fulfilled desire. ||137.87||

O traveller in the chariot of the Sun,
High priestess in the holy fancy's shrine
Who with a magic ritual in earth's house
Worshippest ideal and eternal love,
What is this love thy thought has deified,
This sacred legend and immortal myth? ||140.28||

At last the soul turns to eternal things,
In every shrine it cries for the clasp of God. ||142.14||

A lonely soul passions for the Alone,
The heart that loved man thrills to the love of God,
A body is his chamber and his shrine. ||142.22||

The soul is a figure of the Unmanifest,
The mind labours to think the Unthinkable,
The life to call the Immortal into birth,
The body to enshrine the Illimitable. ||144.42||

tabernacle

But Savitri's heart replied in the dim night:
"My strength is taken from me and given to Death,
Why should I lift my hands to the shut heavens
Or struggle with mute inevitable Fate
Or hope in vain to uplift an ignorant race
Who hug their lot and mock the saviour Light
And see in Mind Wisdom's sole tabernacle,
In its harsh peak and its inconscient base
A rock of safety and an anchor of sleep? ||116.7||

When all thy work in human time is done,
The mind of earth shall be a home of light,
The life of earth a tree growing towards heaven,
The body of earth a tabernacle of God. ||154.11||

A soul shall wake in the Inconscient's house;
The mind shall be God-vision's tabernacle,
The body intuition's instrument,
And life a channel for God's visible power. ||155.44||

temple

Across the path of the divine Event
The huge foreboding mind of Night, alone
In her unlit temple of eternity,
Lay stretched immobile upon Silence' marge. ||1.2||

As in a mystic and dynamic dance
A priestess of immaculate ecstasies
Inspired and ruled from Truth's revealing vault
Moves in some prophet cavern of the gods,
A heart of silence in the hands of joy
Inhabited with rich creative beats
A body like a parable of dawn

That seemed a niche for veiled divinity
Or golden temple door to things beyond. ||3.33||

Even when we fail to look into our souls
Or lie embedded in earthly consciousness,
Still have we parts that grow towards the Light,
Yet are there luminous tracts and heavens serene
And Eldoradoes of splendour and ecstasy
And temples to the Godhead none can see. ||10.9||

So it towered up to heights intangible
And disappeared in the hushed conscious Vast
As climbs a storeyed temple-tower to heaven
Built by the aspiring soul of man to live
Near to his dream of the Invisible. ||26.3||

Insignificant architects of low-built lives
And engineers of interest and desire,
Out of crude earthiness and muddy thrills
And coarse reactions of material nerve
They build our huddled structures of self-will
And the ill-lighted mansions of our thought,
Or with the ego's factories and marts
Surround the beautiful temple of the soul. ||45.25||

All powers of Life towards their godhead tend
In the wideness and the daring of that air,
Each builds its temple and expands its cult,
And Sin too there is a divinity. ||51.21||

Adepts of the illusion and the mask,
The artificers of Nature's fall and pain
Have built their altars of triumphant Night
In the clay temple of terrestrial life. ||63.8||

Here too its bud is born in human breasts;
Then by a touch, a presence or a voice
The world is turned into a temple ground
And all discloses the unknown Beloved. ||73.10||

Or from a far harmonious distance heard
The tinkling pace of a long caravan
It seemed at times, or a vast forest's hymn,
The solemn reminder of a temple gong,
A bee-croon honey-drunk in summer isles
Ardent with ecstasy in a slumberous noon,
Or the far anthem of a pilgrim sea. ||75.13||

Its Power that makes the unknowable near and true,
In the temple of the ideal shrined the One:
It peopled thought and mind and happy sense
Filled with bright aspects of the might of God
And living persons of the one Supreme,
The speech that voices the ineffable,
The ray revealing unseen Presences,
The virgin forms through which the Formless shines,
The Word that ushers divine experience
And the Ideas that crowd the Infinite. ||86.14||

Her mind sat high pouring its golden beams,
Her heart was a crowded temple of delight. ||97.12||

Advancing amid tall heaven-pillaring trees,
Apparelled in her flickering-coloured robe,
She seemed burning towards the eternal realms
A bright moved torch of incense and of flame
That from the sky-roofed temple-soil of earth
A pilgrim hand lifts in an invisible shrine. ||98.30||

At first her path ran far through peopled tracts:
Admitted to the lion eye of States
And theatres of the loud act of man,
Her carven chariot with its fretted wheels
Threaded through clamorous marts and sentinel towers
Past figured gates and high dream-sculptured fronts
And gardens hung in the sapphire of the skies,
Pillared assembly halls with armoured guards,
Small fanes where one calm Image watched man's life
And temples hewn as if by exiled gods
To imitate their lost eternity. ||99.16||

Or near to a lion river's tawny mane
And trees that worshipped on a praying shore,
A domed and templed air's serene repose
Beckoned to her hurrying wheels to stay their speed. ||100.3||

Here were disclosed to her the mystic courts,
The lurking doors of beauty and surprise,
The wings that murmur in the golden house,
The temple of sweetness and the fiery aisle. ||101.21||

A nave of trees enshrined the hermit thatch,
The new deep covert of her felicity,
Preferred to heaven her soul's temple and home. ||105.9||

As if in some Elysian occult depth,
Truth's last retreat from thought's profaning touch,
As if in a rock-temple's solitude hid,
God's refuge from an ignorant worshipping world,
It lay withdrawn even from life's inner sense,
Receding from the entangled heart's desire. ||125.20||

As in a flash from a supernal light,
A living image of the original Power,
A face, a form came down into her heart
And made of it its temple and pure abode. ||127.5||

In the slow process of the evolving spirit,
In the brief stade between a death and birth
A first perfection's stage is reached at last;
Out of the wood and stone of our nature's stuff
A temple is shaped where the high gods could live. ||127.30||

But still in its lone niche of templed strength
Motionless, her flame-bright spirit, mute, erect,
Burned like a torch-fire from a windowed room
Pointing against the darkness' sombre breast. ||137.5||

Not he who has reared his temple in my thoughts
And made his sacred floor my human heart. ||137.91||

Intangible, remote, for ever pure,
A sovereign of its own brilliant void,
Unwillingly it descends to earthly air
To inhabit a white temple in man's heart:
In his heart it shines rejected by his life. ||140.19||

Eternal mountains ridge on gleaming ridge
Whose lines were graved as on a sapphire plate
And etched the borders of heaven's lustrous noon
Climbed like piled temple stairs and from their heads
Of topless meditation heard below
The approach of a blue pilgrim multitude
And listened to a great arriving voice
Of the wide travel hymn of timeless seas. ||140.15||

The Immanent shall be the witness God
Watching on his many-petalled lotus-throne,
His actionless being and his silent might
Ruling earth-nature by eternity's law,
A thinker waking the Inconscient's world,
An immobile centre of many infinitudes
In his thousand-pillared temple by Time's sea. ||155.34||

My adoration mastered, my desire
Bent down to make its subject, my daring clasped,
Claiming by body and soul my life's estate,
Rapture's possession, love's sweet property,
A statue of silence in my templed spirit,
A yearning godhead and a golden bride. ||157.29||

Man the Builder

keel

On a commissioned keel his merchant hull
Serves the world's commerce in the riches of Time
Severing the foam of a great land-locked sea
To reach unknown harbour lights in distant climes
And open markets for life's opulent arts,
Rich bales, carved statuettes, hued canvases,
And jewelled toys brought for an infant's play
And perishable products of hard toil
And transient splendours won and lost by the days. ||17.7||

The sun and moon are lights upon my path;
Air was invented for my lungs to breathe,
Conditioned as a wide and wallless space
For my winged chariot's wheels to cleave a road,
The sea was made for me to swim and sail
And bear my golden commerce on its back:
It laughs cloven by my pleasure's gliding keel,
I laugh at its black stare of fate and death. ||123.37||

prow

His prow pushes towards undiscovered shores,
He chances on unimagined continents:
A seeker of the islands of the Blest,
He leaves the last lands, crosses the ultimate seas,

He turns to eternal things his symbol quest;
Life changes for him its time-constructed scenes,
Its images veiling infinity. ||17.9||

On our life's prow that breaks the waves of Time
No signal light of hope has gleamed in vain. ||142.95||

In those far-lapsing symphonies she could hear
Breaking through enchantments of the ravished sense,
The lyric voyage of a divine soul
Mid spume and laughter tempting with its prow
The charm of innocent Circean isles,
Adventures without danger beautiful
In lands where siren Wonder sings its lures
From rhythmic rocks in ever-foaming seas. ||148.28||

ship

His fragile ship conveys through the sea of years
An incognito of the Imperishable. ||5.15||

As smoothly glides a ship nearing its port,
Ignorant of embargo and blockade,
Confident of entrance and the visa's seal,
It came to the silent city of the brain
Towards its accustomed and expectant quay,
But met a barring will, a blow of Force
And sank vanishing in the immensity. ||129.52||

The wise think with the cycles, they hear the tread
Of far-off things; patient, unmoved they keep
Their dangerous wisdom in their depths restrained,
Lest man's frail days into the unknown should sink
Dragged like a ship by bound leviathan
Into the abyss of his stupendous seas. ||145.16||

Design and Construction of God and Man

city

Late will he know, opening the mystic script,
Whether to a blank port in the Unseen
He goes, or armed with her fiat, to discover
A new mind and body in the city of God
And enshrine the Immortal in his glory's house
And make the finite one with Infinity. ||17.21||

Only another labyrinthine house
Of creatures and their doings and events,
A city of the traffic of bound souls,
A market of creation and her wares
Was offered to the labouring mind and heart. ||54.29||

He saw a city of ancient Ignorance
Founded upon a soil that knew not Light. ||57.3||

Amidst earth's mist and fog and mud and stone
It still remembers its exalted sphere
And the high city of its splendid birth. ||70.25||

A scout of victory in a vigil tower,
Her aspiration called high destiny down;
A silent warrior paced in her city of strength
Inviolate, guarding Truth's diamond throne. ||94.45||

For it has read and broken the hidden seals,
It has drunk of the Immortal's wells of joy,
It has looked across the jewel bars of heaven,
It has entered the aspiring Secrecy,
It sees beyond terrestrial common things
And communes with the Powers that build the worlds,
Till through the shining gates and mystic streets
Of the city of lapis lazuli and pearl
Proud deeds step forth a rank and march of gods. ||106.46||

In the malignant hollows of the world,
In its subconscient cavern-passages
Ambushed they lie waiting their hour to leap,
Surrounding with danger the sieged city of life:
Admitted into the citadel of man's days
They mine his force and maim or suddenly kill.
As smoothly glides a ship nearing its port,
Ignorant of embargo and blockade,
Confident of entrance and the visa's seal,
It came to the silent city of the brain
Towards its accustomed and expectant quay,
But met a barring will, a blow of Force
And sank vanishing in the immensity. ||129.52||

cities

A pride in evil hugged its wretchedness;
A misery haunting splendour pressed those fell
Dun suburbs of the cities of dream-life. ||58.6||

A lone discoverer in these menacing realms
Guarded like termite cities from the sun,
Oppressed mid crowd and tramp and noise and flare,
Passing from dusk to deeper dangerous dusk,
He wrestled with powers that snatched from mind its light
And smote from him their clinging influences. ||60.1||

Each stone was a keen edge of ruthless force
And glued with the chilled blood from tortured breasts;
The dry gnarled trees stood up like dying men
Stiffened into a pose of agony,
And from each window peered an ominous priest
Chanting Te Deums for slaughter's crowning grace,
Cities uprooted, blasted human homes,
Burned writhen bodies, the bombshell's massacre. ||64.13||

Around him was a light of conscious suns
And a brooding gladness of great symbol things;
To meet him crowded plains of brilliant calm,
Mountains and violet valleys of the Blest,
Deep glens of joy and crooning waterfalls
And woods of quivering purple solitude;
Below him lay like gleaming jewelled thoughts
Rapt dreaming cities of Gandharva kings. ||65.9||

These unfamiliar spaces on her way
Were known and neighbours to a sense within;
Landscapes recurred like lost forgotten fields,
Cities and rivers and plains her vision claimed
Like slow-recurring memories in front,
The stars at night were her past's brilliant friends,
The winds murmured to her of ancient things
And she met nameless comrades loved by her once. ||99.4||

A couchant earth wakened in its dumb muse
Looked up at her from a vast indolence:
Hills wallowing in a bright haze, large lands
That lolled at ease beneath the summer heavens,
Region on region spacious in the sun,
Cities like chrysolites in the wide blaze
And yellow rivers pacing, lion-maned,
Led to the Shalwa marches' emerald line,
A happy front to iron vastnesses
And austere peaks and titan solitudes. ||114.8||

A straining taut and dire besieged her heart;
Heavy her sense grew with a dangerous load,
And sadder, greater sounds were in her ears,
And through stern breakings of the lambent glare
Her vision caught a hurry of driving plains
And cloudy mountains and wide tawny streams,
And cities climbed in minarets and towers
Towards an unavailing changeless sky:
Long quays and ghauts and harbours white with sails
Challenged her sight awhile and then were gone. ||143.4||

Around, the deathless nations moved and spoke,
Souls of a luminous celestial joy,
Faces of stark beauty, limbs of the moulded Ray;
In cities cut like gems of conscious stone
And wonderful pastures and on gleaming coasts
Bright forms were seen, eternity's luminous tribes. ||148.19||

hamlet

Hamlet and village saw the fate-van pass,
Homes of a life bent to the soil it ploughs
For sustenance of its short and passing days
That, transient, keep their old repeated course
Unchanging in the circle of a sky
Which alters not above our mortal toil. ||99.18||

parish

This surely is best to pactise with my fate
And follow close behind my lover's steps
And pass through night from twilight to the sun
Across the tenebrous river that divides
The adjoining parishes of earth and heaven. ||116.12||

suburbs

A pride in evil hugged its wretchedness;
A misery haunting splendour pressed those fell
Dun suburbs of the cities of dream-life. ||58.6||

town

In armoured town or gardened pleasure-walks,
Even in distance closer than her thoughts,
Body to body near, soul near to soul,
Moving as if by a common breath and will,
They were tied in the single circling of their days
Together by love's unseen atmosphere,
Inseparable like the earth and sky. ||128.13||

village

Hamlet and village saw the fate-van pass,
Homes of a life bent to the soil it ploughs
For sustenance of its short and passing days
That, transient, keep their old repeated course
Unchanging in the circle of a sky
Which alters not above our mortal toil. ||99.18||

Art and Artistry, The Designs of God, Man and other powers.

art

Original and supernal Immanence
Of which all Nature's process is the art,
The cosmic Worker set his secret hand
To turn this frail mud-engine to heaven-use. ||50.30||

Inspired by silence and the closed eyes' sight
His force could work with a new luminous art
On the crude material from which all is made
And the refusal of Inertia's mass
And the grey front of the world's Ignorance
And nescient Matter and the huge error of life. ||7.20||

Out of the rich wonders and the intricate whorls
Of the spirit's dance with Matter as its mask
The balance of the world's design grew clear,
Its symmetry of self-arranged effects
Managed in the deep perspectives of the soul,
And the realism of its illusive art,
Its logic of infinite intelligence,
Its magic of a changing eternity. ||8.17||

A brighter heavenlier sun must soon illume
This dusk room with its dark internal stair,
The infant soul in its small nursery school

Mid objects meant for a lesson hardly learned
Outgrow its early grammar of intellect
And its imitation of Earth-Nature's art,
Its earthly dialect to God-language change,
In living symbols study Reality
And learn the logic of the Infinite. ||19.3||

All worlds she makes the partners of her deeds,
Accomplices of her mighty violence,
Her daring leaps into the impossible:
From every source she has taken her cunning means,
She draws from the free-love marriage of the planes
Elements for her creation's tour-de-force:
A wonder-weft of knowledge incalculable,
A compendium of divine invention's feats
She has combined to make the unreal true
Or liberate suppressed reality:
In her unhedged Circean wonderland
Pell-mell she shepherds her occult mightinesses;
Her mnemonics of the craft of the Infinite,
Jets of the screened subliminal's caprice,
Tags of the gramarye of Inconscience,
Freedom of a sovereign Truth without a law,
Thoughts that were born in the immortals' world,
Oracles that break out from behind the shrine,
Warnings from the daemonic inner voice
And peeps and lightning-leaps of prophecy
And intimations to the inner ear,
Abrupt interventions stark and absolute
And the superconscient's unaccountable acts,
Have woven her balanced web of miracles
And the weird technique of her tremendous art. ||22.20||

Earth's eyes half see, her forces half create;
Her rarest works are copies of heaven's art. ||30.8||

To copy on earth's copies is his art. ||30.11||

An enigmatic labour of the Spirit,
An exact machine of which none knows the use,
An art and ingenuity without sense,
This minute elaborate orchestrated life
For ever plays its motiveless symphonies. ||45.2||

A magic flowed as if of moving scenes
That kept awhile their fugitive delicacy
Of sparing lines limned by an abstract art
In a rare scanted light with faint dream-brush
On a silver background of incertitude. ||49.9||

Yet by her skill the impossible has been done:
She follows her sublime irrational plan,
Invents devices of her magic art
To find new bodies for the Infinite
And images of the Unimaginable;
She has lured the Eternal into the arms of Time. ||50.20||

Or Beauty shines on them like a wandering star;
Too far to reach, passionate they follow her light;
In Art and Life they catch the All-Beautiful's ray
And make the world their radiant treasure house:
Even common figures are with marvel robed;
A charm and greatness locked in every hour
Awakes the joy which sleeps in all things made. ||51.25||

Alone the God-given hymn escapes her art
That came with her from her spiritual home
But stopped half-way and failed, a silent word
Awake in some deep pause of waiting worlds,
A murmur suspended in eternity's hush:
But no breath comes from the supernal peace:
A sumptuous interlude occupies the ear
And the heart listens and the soul consents;

An evanescent music it repeats
Wasting on transience Time's eternity. ||53.32||

In booths of sin and night-repairs of vice
Styled infamies of the body's concupiscence
And sordid imaginations etched in flesh,
Turned lust into a decorative art:
Abusing Nature's gift her pervert skill
Immortalised the sown grain of living death,
In a mud goblet poured the bacchic wine,
To a satyr gave the thyrsus of a god. ||58.11||

Her craft ingenious in monstrosity,
Impatient of all natural shape and poise,
A gape of nude exaggerated lines,
Gave caricature a stark reality,
And art-parades of weird distorted forms,
And gargoyle masks obscene and terrible
Trampled to tormented postures the torn sense.
A new aesthesis of Inferno's art
That trained the mind to love what the soul hates,
Imposed allegiance on the quivering nerves
And forced the unwilling body to vibrate. ||58.16||

On earth by the will of this Arch-Intelligence
A bodiless energy put on Matter's robe;
Proton and photon served the imager Eye
To change things subtle into a physical world
And the invisible appeared as shape
And the impalpable was felt as mass:
Magic of percept joined with concept's art
And lent to each object an interpreting name:
Idea was disguised in a body's artistry,
And by a strange atomic law's mystique
A frame was made in which the sense would put
Its symbol picture of the universe. ||66.26||

A specialist of logic's hard machine
Imposed its rigid artifice on the soul;
An aide of the inventor intellect,
It cut Truth into manageable bits
That each might have his ration of thought-food,
Then new-built Truth's slain body by its art:
A robot exact and serviceable and false
Displaced the spirit's finer view of things:
A polished engine did the work of a god. ||66.33||

On all sides runs as if in a cosmic mosque
Tracing the scriptural verses of her laws
The daedal of her patterned arabesques,
Art of her wisdom, artifice of her lore. ||68.48||

This art, this artifice are her only stock.
A shoreless sweep was lent to the mortal's acts,
And art and beauty sprang from the human depths;
Nature and soul vied in nobility. ||95.4||

These things she took in as her nature's food,
But these alone could fill not her wide Self:
A human seeking limited by its gains,
To her they seemed the great and early steps
Hazardous of a young discovering spirit
Which saw not yet by its own native light;
It tapped the universe with testing knocks
Or stretched to find Truth-mind's divining rod;
A growing out there was to numberless sides,
But not the widest seeing of the soul,
Not yet the vast direct immediate touch,
Nor yet the art and wisdom of the Gods. ||95.15||

I strove to find its hints through Beauty and Art,
But Form cannot unveil the indwelling Power;
Only it throws its symbols at our hearts. ||103.64||

A treasure misspent or cheaply, fruitlessly sold
In the bazar of a blind destiny,
A gift of priceless values from Time's gods
Lost or mislaid in an uncaring world,
Life is a marvel missed, an art gone wry;
A seeker in a dark and obscure place,
An ill-armed warrior facing dreadful odds,
An imperfect worker given a baffling task,
An ignorant judge of problems Ignorance made,
Its heavenward flights reach closed and keyless gates,
Its glorious outbursts peter out in mire. ||107.25||

A miracle structure of the eternal Mage,
Matter its mystery hides from its own eyes,
A scripture written out in cryptic signs,
An occult document of the All-Wonderful's art.
Then larger dawns arrive and Wisdom's pomps
Cross through the being's dim, half-lighted fields;
Philosophy climbs up Thought's cloud-bank peaks
And Science tears out Nature's occult powers,
Enormous jinns who serve a dwarf's small needs,
Exposes the sealed minutiae of her art
And conquers her by her own captive force. ||141.56||

Life brings into the earthly creature's days
A tongue of glory from a higher sphere:
It deepens in his musings and his Art,
It leaps at the splendour of some perfect word,
It exults in his high resolves and noble deeds,
Wanders in his errors, dares the abyss's brink,
It climbs in his climbings, wallows in his fall. ||142.11||

In him the architect of the visible world,
At once the art and artist of his works,
Spirit and seer and thinker of things seen,

Virât, who lights his camp-fires in the suns
And the star-entangled ether is his hold,
Expressed himself with Matter for his speech:
Objects are his letters, forces are his words,
Events are the crowded history of his life,
And sea and land are the pages of his tale,
Matter is his means and his spiritual sign;
He hangs the thought upon a lash's lift,
In the current of the blood makes flow the soul. ||149.15||

On a commissioned keel his merchant hull
Serves the world's commerce in the riches of Time
Severing the foam of a great land-locked sea
To reach unknown harbour lights in distant climes
And open markets for life's opulent arts,
Rich bales, carved statuettes, hued canvases,
And jewelled toys brought for an infant's play
And perishable products of hard toil
And transient splendours won and lost by the days. ||117.7||

Yet through it all I have kept my balanced thought;
I have studied my being, I have examined the world,
I have grown a master of the arts of life. ||123.48||

As when pale lightnings tear a tortured sky,
High overhead a cloud-rimmed series flared
Chasing like smoke from a red funnel driven,
The forced creations of an ignorant Mind:
Drifting she saw like pictured fragments flee
Phantoms of human thought and baffled hopes,
The shapes of Nature and the arts of man,
Philosophies and disciplines and laws,
And the dead spirit of old societies,
Constructions of the Titan and the worm. ||143.9||

If something great awakes, too frail his pitch
To reveal its zenith tension of delight,
His thought to eternise its ephemeral soar,
Art's brilliant gleam is a pastime for his eyes,
A thrill that smites the nerves is music's spell. ||46.10||

A spirit that is a flame of God abides,
A fiery portion of the Wonderful,
Artist of his own beauty and delight,
Immortal in our mortal poverty. ||5.16||

In the mystery of her cosmic ignorance,
In the insoluble riddle of her play,
A creature made of perishable stuff,
In the pattern she has set for him he moves,
He thinks with her thoughts, with her trouble his bosom heaves;
He seems the thing that she would have him seem,
He is whatever her artist will can make. ||14.12||

Yet some first image of greatness trembles there,
And when the ambiguous crowded parts have met
The many-toned unity to which they moved,
The Artist's joy shall laugh at reason's rules;
The divine intention suddenly shall be seen,
The end vindicate intuition's sure technique. ||26.23||

Its knowledge is our error's starting-point;
Its beauty dons our mud-mask ugliness,
Its artist good begins our evil's tale. ||28.30||

A perfect picture in a perfect frame,
This faery artistry could not keep his will:
Only a moment's fine release it gave;
A careless hour was spent in a slight bliss. ||31.18||

Artists minute of the hues of littleness,
They set the mosaic of Life's comedy
Or plan the trivial tragedy of our days,
Arrange the deed, combine the circumstance
And the fantasia of the moods costume. ||45.26||

On earth by the will of this Arch-Intelligence
A bodiless energy put on Matter's robe;
Proton and photon served the imager Eye
To change things subtle into a physical world
And the invisible appeared as shape
And the impalpable was felt as mass:
Magic of percept joined with concept's art
And lent to each object an interpreting name:
Idea was disguised in a body's artistry,
And by a strange atomic law's mystique
A frame was made in which the sense would put
Its symbol picture of the universe. ||66.26||

For here was no firm clue and no sure road;
High-climbing pathways closed in the unknown;
An artist sight constructed the Beyond
In contrary patterns and conflicting hues;
A part-experience fragmented the Whole. ||74.34||

At hide and seek on a Mother-Wisdom's breast,
An artist teeming with her world-idea,
She never could exhaust its numberless thoughts
And vast adventure into thinking shapes
And trial and lure of a new living's dreams. ||86.20||

There Matter is the Spirit's firm density,
An artistry of glad outwardness of self,
A treasure-house of lasting images
Where sense can build a world of pure delight:
The home of a perpetual happiness,
It lodged the hours as in a pleasant inn. ||86.22||

O Truth defended in thy secret sun,
Voice of her mighty musings in shut heavens
On things withdrawn within her luminous depths,
O Wisdom-Splendour, Mother of the universe,
Creatrix, the Eternal's artist Bride,
Linger not long with thy transmuting hand
Pressed vainly on one golden bar of Time,
As if Time dare not open its heart to God. ||90.36||

There came the gift of a revealing hour:
He saw through depths that reinterpret all,
Limited not now by the dull body's eyes,
New-found through an arch of clear discovery,
This intimation of the world's delight,
This wonder of the divine Artist's make
Carved like a nectar-cup for thirsty gods,
This breathing Scripture of the Eternal's joy,
This net of sweetness woven of aureate fire. ||98.31||

O rubies of silence, lips from which there stole
Low laughter, music of tranquillity,
Star-lustrous eyes awake in sweet large night
And limbs like fine-linked poems made of gold
Stanzaed to glimmering curves by artist gods,
Depart where love and destiny call your charm. ||98.48||

Awake to Nature, vague as yet to life,
The eager prisoner from the Infinite,
The immortal wrestler in its mortal house,
Its pride, power, passion of a striving God,
It saw this image of veiled deity,
This thinking master creature of the earth,
This last result of the beauty of the stars,
But only saw like fair and common forms
The artist spirit needs not for its work
And puts aside in memory's shadowy rooms. ||102.21||

But greater spirits this balance can reverse
And make the soul the artist of its fate. ||114.4||

I have made real what she never dreamed,
I have seized her powers and harnessed for my work,
I have shaped her metals and new metals made;
I will make glass and raiment out of milk,
Make iron velvet, water unbreakable stone,
Like God in his astuce of artist skill,
Mould from one primal plasm protean forms,
In single nature multitudinous lives,
All that imagination can conceive
In mind intangible, remould anew
In Matter's plastic solid and concrete;
No magic can surpass my magic's skill. ||123.42||

Each shape showed its occult design, unveiled
God's meaning in it for which it was made
And the vivid splendour of his artist thought. ||127.14||

This mind is a dynamic small machine
Producing ceaselessly till it wears out,
With raw material drawn from the outside world,
The patterns sketched out by an artist God. ||129.29||

To the enjoyer of the cosmic scene
His greatness and his littleness equal are,
His magnanimity and meanness hues
Cast on some neutral background of the gods:
The Artist's skill he admires who made the plan,
But not for ever endures this danger game:
Beyond the earth, but meant for delivered earth,
Wisdom and joy prepare their perfect crown:
Truth superhuman calls to thinking man. ||142.13||

A march of universal power in Time,
The harmonic order of self's vastitudes
In cyclic symmetries and metric planes
Harboured a cosmic rapture's revelry
In an endless figuring of the spirit in things
Planned by the artist who has dreamed the worlds;
Of all the beauty and the marvel here,
Of all Time's intricate variety
Eternity was the substance and the source;
Not from a plastic mist of Matter made,
They offered the suggestion of their depths
And opened the great series of their powers. ||148.9||

Impeccable artists of unerring forms,
Magician builders of sound and rhythmic words,
Wind-haired Gundhurvas chanted to the ear
The odes that shape the universal thought,
The lines that tear the veil from Deity's face,
The rhythms that bring the sounds of wisdom's sea. ||148.42||

In him the architect of the visible world,
At once the art and artist of his works,
Spirit and seer and thinker of things seen,
Virât, who lights his camp-fires in the suns
And the star-entangled ether is his hold,
Expressed himself with Matter for his speech:
Objects are his letters, forces are his words,
Events are the crowded history of his life,
And sea and land are the pages of his tale,
Matter is his means and his spiritual sign;
He hangs the thought upon a lash's lift,
In the current of the blood makes flow the soul. ||149.15||

caricature

Her craft ingenious in monstrosity,
Impatient of all natural shape and poise,
A gape of nude exaggerated lines,
Gave caricature a stark reality,
And art-parades of weird distorted forms,
And gargoyle masks obscene and terrible
Trampled to tormented postures the torn sense. ||58.13||

carved

Sri Aurobindo's use of the word 'carve' is used occasionally in the literal
sense as when he is speaking of Savitri's chariot or Satyavan's carvings
'out of wood and stone', or the 'white carved pillars' of the palace in
Madra, but more often in senses that are supraphysical, mystical,
informed with the vision and touch of higher worlds bringing them down
into us when read aloud.

There knowledge needs not words to embody Idea;
Idea seeking a house in boundlessness,
Weary of its homeless immortality,
Asks not in thought's carved brilliant cell to rest
Whose single window's clipped outlook on things
Sees only a little arc of God's vast sky. ||6.48||

The war of thoughts that fathers the universe,
The clash of forces struggling to prevail
In the tremendous shock that lights a star
As in the building of a grain of dust,
The grooves that turn their dumb ellipse in space
Ploughed by the seeking of the world's desire,
The long regurgitations in Time's flood,
The torment edging the dire force of lust
That wakes kinetic in earth's dullard slime
And carves a personality out of mud,
The sorrow by which Nature's hunger is fed,

The oestrus which creates with fire of pain,
The fate that punishes virtue with defeat,
The tragedy that destroys long happiness,
The weeping of Love, the quarrel of the Gods,
Ceased in a truth which lives in its own light. ||6.54||

On a commissioned keel his merchant hull
Serves the world's commerce in the riches of Time
Severing the foam of a great land-locked sea
To reach unknown harbour lights in distant climes
And open markets for life's opulent arts,
Rich bales, carved statuettes, hued canvases,
And jewelled toys brought for an infant's play
And perishable products of hard toil
And transient splendours won and lost by the days. ||17.7||

An almighty occultist erects in space
This seeming outward world which tricks the sense;
He weaves his hidden threads of consciousness,
He builds bodies for his shapeless energy;
Out of the unformed and vacant Vast he has made
His sorcery of solid images,
His magic of formative number and design,
The fixed irrational links none can annul,
This criss-cross tangle of invisible laws;
His infallible rules, his covered processes,
Achieve unerringly an inexplicable
Creation where our error carves dead frames
Of knowledge for a living ignorance. ||22.7||

As if from Matter's plinth and viewless base
To a top as viewless, a carved sea of worlds
Climbing with foam-maned waves to the Supreme
Ascended towards breadths immeasurable;
It hoped to soar into the Ineffable's reign:
A hundred levels raised it to the Unknown. ||26.2||

Astonished by the unaccustomed glow,
As if immanent in the shadows started up
Imps with wry limbs and carved beast visages,
Sprite prompters goblin-wizened or faery-small,
And genii fairer but unsouled and poor
And fallen beings, their heavenly portion lost,
And errant divinities trapped in Time's dust. ||43.9||

The mind learns and knows not, turning its back to truth;
It studies surface laws by surface thought,
Life's steps surveys and Nature's process sees,
Not seeing for what she acts or why we live;
It marks her tireless care of just device,
Her patient intricacy of fine detail,
The ingenious spirit's brave inventive plan
In her great futile mass of endless works,
Adds purposeful figures to her purposeless sum,
Its gabled storeys piles, its climbing roofs
On the close-carved foundations she has laid,
Imagined citadels reared in mythic air
Or mounts a stair of dream to a mystic moon:
Transient creations point and hit the sky:
A world-conjecture's scheme is laboured out
On the dim floor of mind's incertitude,
Or painfully built a fragmentary whole. ||45.3||

Behind appeared a grey carved mask of Night
Watching the birth of all created things. ||55.6||

At will she spaces in thin air of mind
Like maps in the school-house of intellect hung,
Forcing wide Truth into a narrow scheme,
Her numberless warring strict philosophies;
Out of Nature's body of phenomenon
She carves with Thought's keen edge in rigid lines
Like rails for the World-Magician's power to run,
Her sciences precise and absolute. ||68.47||

The All-containing was contained in form,
Oneness was carved into units measurable,
The limitless built into a cosmic sum:
Unending Space was beaten into a curve,
Indivisible Time into small minutes cut,
The infinitesimal massed to keep secure
The mystery of the Formless cast into form. ||71.15||

Or else, a faithful consort of his mind
Assenting to his nature and his will,
She sanctions and inspires his words and acts
Prolonging their resonance through the listening ears,
Companion and recorder of his march
Crossing a brilliant tract of thought and life
Carved out of the eternity of Time. ||72.3||

In a human breast her occult presence lived;
He carved from his own self his figure of her:
She shaped her body to a mind's embrace. ||72.11||

There came the gift of a revealing hour:
He saw through depths that reinterpret all,
Limited not now by the dull body's eyes,
New-found through an arch of clear discovery,
This intimation of the world's delight,
This wonder of the divine Artist's make
Carved like a nectar-cup for thirsty gods,
This breathing Scripture of the Eternal's joy,
This net of sweetness woven of aureate fire. ||98.31||

At first her path ran far through peopled tracts:
Admitted to the lion eye of States
And theatres of the loud act of man,
Her carven chariot with its fretted wheels
Threaded through clamorous marts and sentinel towers
Past figured gates and high dream-sculptured fronts

And gardens hung in the sapphire of the skies,
Pillared assembly halls with armoured guards,
Small fanes where one calm Image watched man's life
And temples hewn as if by exiled gods
To imitate their lost eternity.　　　　　　　　　||99.16||

As floats a sunbeam through a shady place,
The golden virgin in her carven car
Came gliding among meditation's seats.　　　　||100.1||

I carved my vision out of wood and stone;
I caught the echoes of a word supreme
And metred the rhythm beats of infinity
And listened through music for the eternal Voice.　　||103.38||

Then down she came from her high carven car
Descending with a soft and faltering haste;
Her many-hued raiment glistening in the light
Hovered a moment over the wind-stirred grass,
Mixed with a glimmer of her body's ray
Like lovely plumage of a settling bird.　　　　||104.3||

Once more she mounted on the carven car
And under the ardour of a fiery noon
Less bright than the splendour of her thoughts and dreams
She sped swift-reined, swift-hearted but still saw
In still lucidities of sight's inner world
Through the cool scented wood's luxurious gloom
On shadowy paths between great rugged trunks
Pace towards a tranquil clearing Satyavan.　　||105.8||

But Aswapathy answered to the seer;
His listening mind had marked the dubious close,
An ominous shadow felt behind the words,
But calm like one who ever sits facing Fate

Here mid the dangerous contours of earth's life,
He answered covert thought with guarded speech:
"O deathless sage who knowest all things here,
If I could read by the ray of my own wish
Through the carved shield of symbol images
Which thou hast thrown before thy heavenly mind
I might see the steps of a young godlike life
Happily beginning luminous-eyed on earth;
Between the Unknowable and the Unseen
Born on the borders of two wonder-worlds,
It flames out symbols of the Infinite
And lives in a great light of inner suns. ||106.45||

The past receded and the future neared:
Far now behind lay Madra's spacious halls,
The white carved pillars, the cool dim alcoves,
The tinged mosaic of the crystal floors,
The towered pavilions, the wind-rippled pools
And gardens humming with the murmur of bees,
Forgotten soon or a pale memory
The fountain's plash in the wide stone-bound pool,
The thoughtful noontide's brooding solemn trance,
The colonnade's dream grey in the quiet eve,
The slow moonrise gliding in front of Night. ||114.10||

There one stood forth who bore authority
On an important brow and held a rod;
Command was incarnate in his gesture and tone;
Tradition's petrified wisdom carved his speech,
His sentences savoured the oracle. ||120.7||

Into dim spiritual somnolence they break
Or shed wide wonder on our waking self,
Ideas that haunt us with their radiant tread,
Dreams that are hints of unborn Reality,
Strange goddesses with deep-pooled magical eyes,

Strong wind-haired gods carrying harps of hope,
Great moon-hued visions gliding through gold air,
Aspiration's sun-dream head and star-carved limbs,
Emotions making common hearts sublime. ||121.3||

Here on a boulder carved like a huge throne
A Woman sat in gold and purple sheen,
Armed with the trident and the thunderbolt,
Her feet upon a couchant lion's back. ||123.4||

An awful dimness wrapped the great rock-doors
Carved in the massive stone of Matter's trance. ||125.22||

Then silently she rose and, service done,
Bowed down to the great goddess simply carved
By Satyavan upon a forest stone. ||133.4||

Enigma of the Inconscient's sculptural sleep,
Symbols of the approach to darkness old
And monuments of her titanic reign,
Opening to depths like dumb appalling jaws
That wait a traveller down a haunted path
Attracted to a mystery that slays,
They watched across her road, cruel and still;
Sentinels they stood of dumb Necessity,
Mute heads of vigilant and sullen gloom,
Carved muzzle of a dim enormous world. ||136.24||

Heaven ever young and earth too firm and old
Delay the heart by immobility:
Their raptures of creation last too long,
Their bold formations are too absolute;
Carved by an anguish of divine endeavour
They stand up sculptured on the eternal hills,
Or quarried from the living rocks of God
Win immortality by perfect form. ||139.13||

A solid image of reality
Carved out being to prop the works of Time;
Matter on the firm earth sits strong and sure. ||140.83||

This universe an old enchantment guards;
Its objects are carved cups of World-Delight
Whose charmed wine is some deep soul's rapture-drink:
The All-Wonderful has packed heaven with his dreams,
He has made blank ancient Space his marvel-house;
He spilled his spirit into Matter's signs:
His fires of grandeur burn in the great sun,
He glides through heaven shimmering in the moon;
He is beauty carolling in the fields of sound;
He chants the stanzas of the odes of Wind;
He is silence watching in the stars at night;
He wakes at dawn and calls from every bough,
Lies stunned in the stone and dreams in flower and tree. ||142.5||

Then like an anthem from the heart's lucent cave
A voice soared up whose magic sound could turn
The poignant weeping of the earth to sobs
Of rapture and her cry to spirit song:
"O human image of the deathless word,
How hast thou seen beyond the topaz walls
The gleaming sisters of the divine gate,
Summoned the genii of their wakeful sleep,
And under revelation's arches forced
The carved thought-shrouded doors to swing apart,
Unlocked the avenues of spiritual sight
And taught[6] the entries of a heavenlier state
To thy rapt soul that bore the golden key? ||150.1||

carving

An adjunct glory and a symbol self,
The body was delivered to the soul,—
An immortal point of power, a block of poise

In a cosmicity's wide formless surge,
A conscious edge of the Transcendent's might
Carving perfection from a bright world-stuff,
It figured in it a universe's sense. ||78.34||

The architecture of the Infinite
Discovered here its inward-musing shapes
Captured into wide breadths of soaring stone:
Music brought down celestial yearnings, song
Held the merged heart absorbed in rapturous depths,
Linking the human with the cosmic cry;
The world-interpreting movements of the dance
Moulded idea and mood to a rhythmic sway
And posture; crafts minute in subtle lines
Eternised a swift moment's memory
Or showed in a carving's sweep, a cup's design
The underlying patterns of the unseen:
Poems in largeness cast like moving worlds
And metres surging with the ocean's voice
Translated by grandeurs locked in Nature's heart
But thrown now into a crowded glory of speech
The beauty and sublimity of her forms,
The passion of her moments and her moods
Lifting the human word near to the god's. ||95.13||

Or wherefore did he build my mortal form
And sow in me his bright and proud desires,
If not to achieve, to flower in me, to love,
Carving his human image richly shaped
In thoughts and largenesses and golden powers? ||145.40||

chiaroscuro

A wanderer in a world his thoughts have made,
He turns in a chiaroscuro of error and truth
To find a wisdom that on high is his. ||16.4||

craft, Craftsman,

The Craftsman of the magic stuff of self
Who labours at his high and difficult plan
In the wide workshop of the wonderful world,
Modelled in inward Time his rhythmic parts. ||5.32||

Out of apprenticeship to Ignorance
Wisdom upraised him to her master craft
And made him an arch-mason of the soul,
A builder of the Immortal's secret house,
An aspirant to supernal Timelessness:
Freedom and empire called to him from on high;
Above mind's twilight and life's star-led night
There gleamed the dawn of a spiritual day. ||5.40||

A fine degree in wonder's hierarchy,
The kingdom of subtle Matter's faery craft
Outlined against a sky of vivid hues,
Leaping out of a splendour-trance and haze,
The wizard revelation of its front. ||28.2||

A kindling rapture joins the seer and seen;
The craftsman and the craft grown inly one
Achieve perfection by the magic throb
And passion of their close identity. ||30.34||

Then, for her rebel waking's punishment
Given only hard mechanic Circumstance
As the enginery of her magic craft,
She fashions godlike marvels out of mud;
In the plasm she sets her dumb immortal urge,
Helps the live tissue to think, the closed sense to feel,
Flashes through the frail nerves poignant messages,
In a heart of flesh miraculously loves,
To brute bodies gives a soul, a will, a voice. ||50.47||

A witness overmastered by his scene,
He admired her splendid front of pomp and play
And the marvels of her rich and delicate craft,
And thrilled to the insistence of her cry;
Impassioned he bore the sorceries of her might,
Felt laid on him her abrupt mysterious will,
Her hands that knead fate in their violent grasp,
Her touch that moves, her powers that seize and drive. ||52.21||

Allured by the many-toned marvel of her chant,
Attracted by the witchcraft of her moods
And moved by her casual touch to joy and grief,
He loses himself in her but wins her not. ||53.16||

Her craft ingenious in monstrosity,
Impatient of all natural shape and poise,
A gape of nude exaggerated lines,
Gave caricature a stark reality,
And art-parades of weird distorted forms,
And gargoyle masks obscene and terrible
Trampled to tormented postures the torn sense. ||58.13||

Thus worked the Power upon the growing world;
Its subtle craft withheld the full-orbed blaze,
Cherished the soul's childhood and on fictions fed
Far richer in their sweet and nectarous sap
Nourishing its immature divinity
Than the staple or dry straw of Reason's tilth,
Its heaped fodder of innumerable facts,
Plebian fare on which today we thrive. ||66.38||

Invincibly their craft devised for use
The magic of sequent number and sign's spell,
Design's miraculous potency was caught
Laden with beauty and significance

And by the determining mandate of their gaze
Figure and quality equating joined
In an inextricable identity. ||71.16||

The architecture of the Infinite
Discovered here its inward-musing shapes
Captured into wide breadths of soaring stone:
Music brought down celestial yearnings, song
Held the merged heart absorbed in rapturous depths,
Linking the human with the cosmic cry;
The world-interpreting movements of the dance
Moulded idea and mood to a rhythmic sway
And posture; crafts minute in subtle lines
Eternised a swift moment's memory
Or showed in a carving's sweep, a cup's design
The underlying patterns of the unseen:
Poems in largeness cast like moving worlds
And metres surging with the ocean's voice
Translated by grandeurs locked in Nature's heart
But thrown now into a crowded glory of speech
The beauty and sublimity of her forms,
The passion of her moments and her moods
Lifting the human word near to the god's. ||95.13||

All else is Nature's craft and this too hers. ||129.32||

A miracle-monger her mechanical craft;
Matter's machine worked out the laws of thought,
Life's engines served the labour of a soul:
The mighty Mother her creation wrought,
A huge caprice self-bound by iron laws,
And shut God into an enigmatic world:
She lulled the Omniscient into nescient sleep,
Omnipotence on Inertia's back she drove,
Trod perfectly with divine unconscious steps
The enormous circle of her wonder-works. ||141.38||

On earth it lingers drinking its deep fill,
Through the symbol of her pleasure and her pain,
Of the grapes of Heaven and the flowers of the Abyss,
Of the flame-stabs and the torment-craft of Hell
And dim fragments of the glory of Paradise.　　||142.8||

Each in its hour eternal claimed went by:
Ideals, systems, sciences, poems, crafts
Tireless there perished and again recurred,
Sought restlessly by some creative Power.　　||143.11||

design, design's

Out of the rich wonders and the intricate whorls
Of the spirit's dance with Matter as its mask
The balance of the world's design grew clear,
Its symmetry of self-arranged effects
Managed in the deep perspectives of the soul,
And the realism of its illusive art,
Its logic of infinite intelligence,
Its magic of a changing eternity.　　||8.17||

In her material order's fixed design
Where all seems sure and even when changed, the same,
Even though the end is left for ever unknown
And ever unstable is life's shifting flow,
His paths are found for him by silent fate;
As stations in the ages' weltering flood
Firm lands appear that tempt and stay awhile,
Then new horizons lure the mind's advance.　　||16.11||

In his world-adventure's crude initial start
Behold him ignorant of his godhead's force,
Timid initiate of its vast design.　　||17.2||

One among many thousands never touched,
Engrossed in the external world's design,
Is chosen by a secret witness Eye
And driven by a pointing hand of Light
Across his soul's unmapped immensitudes. ||20.13||

Incalculable in their wizard modes,
Immediate and invincible in the act,
Her secret strengths native to greater worlds
Lifted above our needy limited scope,
The occult privilege of demigods
And the sure power-pattern of her cryptic signs,
Her diagrams of geometric force,
Her potencies of marvel-fraught design
Courted employment by an earth-nursed might. ||22.4||

An almighty occultist erects in space
This seeming outward world which tricks the sense;
He weaves his hidden threads of consciousness,
He builds bodies for his shapeless energy;
Out of the unformed and vacant Vast he has made
His sorcery of solid images,
His magic of formative number and design,
The fixed irrational links none can annul,
This criss-cross tangle of invisible laws;
His infallible rules, his covered processes,
Achieve unerringly an inexplicable
Creation where our error carves dead frames
Of knowledge for a living ignorance. ||22.7||

His vast design accepts a puny start. ||26.21||

A fragment here is caught of heaven's design;
Else could we never hope for greater life
And ecstasy and glory could not be. ||30.4||

Here mingling in man's heart their tones and hues
Have woven his being's mutable design,
His life a forward-rippling stream in Time,
His nature's constant fixed mobility,
His soul a moving picture's changeful film,
His cosmos-chaos of personality. ||34.20||

In a dwarf model of humanity
Nature now launched the extreme experience
And master-point of her design's caprice,
Luminous result of her half-conscious climb
On rungs twixt her sublimities and grotesques
To massive from infinitesimal shapes,
To a subtle balancing of body and soul,
To an order of intelligent littleness. ||41.6||

If new designs, if richer details grow
And thought is added and more tangled cares,
If little by little it wears a brighter face,
Still even in man the plot is mean and poor. ||46.3||

As quivers with the thought the expressive word,
As yearns the act with the passion of the soul
This world's apparent sensible design
Looks vibrant back to some interior might. ||51.29||

As one who spells illumined characters,
The key-book of a crabbed magician text,
He scanned her subtle tangled weird designs
And the screened difficult theorem of her clues,
Traced in the monstrous sands of desert Time
The thread beginnings of her titan works,
Watched her charade of action for some hint,
Read the No-gestures of her silhouettes,
And strove to capture in their burdened drift

The dance-fantasia of her sequences
Escaping into rhythmic mystery,
A glimmer of fugitive feet on fleeing soil. ||52.6||

As in a fragmentary half-lost design
Life's meanings fled from the pursuing eye. ||53.6||

The thought that gives it sense lives far beyond;
It is not seen in its half-finished design. ||53.8||

A sovereign ruling falsehood, death and grief,
It pressed its fierce hegemony on earth;
Disharmonising the original style
Of the architecture of her fate's design,
It falsified the primal cosmic Will
And bound to struggle and dread vicissitudes
The long slow process of the patient Power. ||62.11||

Adept of clear contrivance and design,
A pensive face and close and peering eyes,
She took her firm and irremovable seat,
The strongest, wisest of the troll-like Three. ||68.37||

Invincibly their craft devised for use
The magic of sequent number and sign's spell,
Design's miraculous potency was caught
Laden with beauty and significance
And by the determining mandate of their gaze
Figure and quality equating joined
In an inextricable identity. ||71.16||

A wisdom read their mind to themselves unknown,
Their anarchy rammed into a formula
And from their giant randomness of Force,
Following the habit of their million paths,
Distinguishing each faintest line and stroke

Of a concealed unalterable design,
Out of the chaos of the Invisible's moods
Derived the calculus of Destiny. ||71.34||

The mighty Mother's whims and lightning moods
Arisen from her all-wise unruled delight
In the freedom of her sweet and passionate breast,
Robbed of their wonder were chained to a cause and aim;
An idol of bronze replaced her mystic shape
That captures the movements of the cosmic vasts,
In the sketch precise of an ideal face
Forgotten was her eyelashes' dream-print
Carrying on their curve infinity's dreams,
Lost the alluring marvel of her eyes;
The surging wave-throbs of her vast sea-heart
They bound to a theorem of ordered beats:
Her deep designs which from herself she had veiled
Bowed self-revealed in their confessional. ||71.37||

Falling upon the surface consciousness,
And in the dream of a mute witness soul
Creating the error of a half-seen world
Where knowledge is a seeking ignorance,
Life's steps a stumbling series without suit,
Its aspect of fortuitous design,
Its equal measure of the true and false
In that immobile and immutable realm
Find no access, no cause, no right to live:
There only reigns the Spirit's motionless power
Poised in itself through still eternity
And its omniscient and omnipotent peace. ||84.6||

A Mind empowered from Truth's immutable seat
Was framed for vision and interpreting act
And instruments were sovereignly designed
To express divinity in terrestrial signs. ||94.12||

The architecture of the Infinite
Discovered here its inward-musing shapes
Captured into wide breadths of soaring stone:
Music brought down celestial yearnings, song
Held the merged heart absorbed in rapturous depths,
Linking the human with the cosmic cry;
The world-interpreting movements of the dance
Moulded idea and mood to a rhythmic sway
And posture; crafts minute in subtle lines
Eternised a swift moment's memory
Or showed in a carving's sweep, a cup's design
The underlying patterns of the unseen:
Poems in largeness cast like moving worlds
And metres surging with the ocean's voice
Translated by grandeurs locked in Nature's heart
But thrown now into a crowded glory of speech
The beauty and sublimity of her forms,
The passion of her moments and her moods
Lifting the human word near to the god's. ||95.13||

A prescient architect of Fate and Chance
Who builds our lives on a foreseen design
The meaning knows and consequence of each step
And watches the inferior stumbling powers. ||99.13||

Although designed like a nectar cup of heaven,
Of heavenly ether made she sought this air,
She too must share the human need of grief
And all her cause of joy transmute to pain. ||112.10||

Each shape showed its occult design, unveiled
God's meaning in it for which it was made
And the vivid splendour of his artist thought. ||127.14||

All seemed a brilliant shadow of itself,
A cosmic film of scenes and images:

The enduring mass and outline of the hills
Was a design sketched on a silent mind
And held to a tremulous false solidity
By constant beats of visionary sight;
The forest with its emerald multitudes
Clothed with its show of hues vague empty Space,
A painting's colours hiding a surface void
That flickered upon dissolution's edge;
The blue heavens, an illusion of the eyes,
Roofed in the mind's illusion of a world. ||130.16||

I, Death, was king and kept my regal state,
Designing my unwilled, unerring plan,
Creating with a calm insentient heart. ||140.98||

Ascending out of the limiting breadths of mind,
They shall discover the world's huge design
And step into the Truth, the Right, the Vast. ||155.20||

Interpreter of a diviner law
And instrument of a supreme design
The higher kind shall lean to lift up man. ||155.56||

draw, drawing, drawn

An image fluttering on the screen of fate
Half-animated for a passing show,
Or a castaway on the ocean of Desire
Flung to the eddies in a ruthless sport
And tossed along the gulfs of Circumstance,
A creature born to bend beneath the yoke,
A chattel and a plaything of Time's lords,
Or one more pawn who comes destined to be pushed
One slow move forward on a measureless board
In the chess-play of the earth-soul with Doom,—
Such is the human figure drawn by Time. ||4.17||

A fearless will for knowledge dared to erase
The lines of safety reason draws that bar
Mind's soar, soul's dive into the Infinite. ||6.2||

There is limned ever retreating from the eyes,
As if in a tenuous misty dream-light drawn,
The outline of a dim mysterious shore. ||17.16||

Immutably coeval with the world,
Circle and end of every hope and toil
Inexorably drawn round thought and act,
The fixed immovable peripheries
Effaced themselves beneath the Incarnate's tread. ||21.14||

An attempt, a drawing half-done is the world's life;
Its lines doubt their concealed significance,
Its curves join not their high-intended close. ||26.22||

A brief companionship with many jars,
A little love and jealousy and hate,
A touch of friendship mid indifferent crowds
Draw his heart-plan on life's diminutive map. ||46.9||

It peers at the Real through the apparent form;
It labours in our mortal mind and sense;
Amid the figures of the Ignorance,
In the symbol pictures drawn by word and thought,
It seeks the truth to which all figures point;
It looks for the source of Light with vision's lamp;
It works to find the doer of all works,
The unfelt Self within who is the guide,
The unknown Self above who is the goal. ||47.8||

Acolytes they wait upon the timeless Power,
The cycle of her works investigate;

Passing her fence of wordless privacy
Their mind could penetrate her occult mind
And draw the diagram of her secret thoughts;
They read the codes and ciphers she had sealed,
Copies they made of all her guarded plans,
For every turn of her mysterious course
Assigned a reason and unchanging rule. ||71.28||

Assessed was the system of the probable,
The hazard of fleeing possibilities,
To account for the Actual's unaccountable sum,
Necessity's logarithmic tables drawn,
Cast into a scheme the triple act of the One. ||71.32||

For the birth and death of the worlds they fixed a date,
The diameter of Infinity was drawn,
Measured the distant arc of the unseen heights
And visualised the plumbless viewless depths
Till all seemed known that in all time could be. ||71.38||

There was nothing there but a schema drawn by sense,
A substitute for eternal mysteries,
A scrawl figure of reality, a plan
And elevation by the architect Word
Imposed upon the semblances of Time. ||74.28||

Infallibly the curves of life are drawn
Following the stream of Time through the unknown;
They are led by a clue the calm immortals keep. ||112.6||

This world was not built with random bricks of chance,
A blind god is not destiny's architect;
A conscious power has drawn the plan of life,
There is a meaning in each curve and line. ||112.41||

All this the spirit concealed had done in her:
A portion of the mighty Mother came
Into her as into its own human part:
Amid the cosmic workings of the Gods
It marked her the centre of a wide-drawn scheme,
Dreamed in the passion of her far-seeing spirit
To mould humanity into God's own shape
And lead this great blind struggling world to light
Or a new world discover or create. ||117.89||

Her spirit seemed the substance of a name,
The world a pictured symbol drawn on self,
A dream of images, a dream of sounds
Built up the semblance of a universe
Or lent to spirit the appearance of a world. ||130.3||

Or if she dwells not within thy mortal heart,
Show me the body of the living Truth
Or draw for me the outline of her face
That I too may obey and worship her. ||146.15||

But still it holds him dangled in its grasp:
It draws its giant circle round its thoughts,
It shuts its heart to the supernal Light,
A high and dazzling limit shines above,
A black and blinding border rules below:
His mind is closed between two firmaments. ||152.22||

Then shall the embodied being live as one
Who is a thought, a will of the Divine,
A mask or robe of his divinity,
An instrument and partner of his Force,
A point or line drawn in the infinite,
A manifest of the Imperishable. ||155.35||

etched

In booths of sin and night-repairs of vice
Styled infamies of the body's concupiscence
And sordid imaginations etched in flesh,
Turned lust into a decorative art:
Abusing Nature's gift her pervert skill
Immortalised the sown grain of living death,
In a mud goblet poured the bacchic wine,
To a satyr gave the thyrsus of a god. ||158.11||

In her visions and deep-etched veridical dreams,
In brief shiftings of the future's heavy screen,
He lay not by a dolorous decree
A victim in the dismal antre of death
Or borne to blissful regions far from her
Forgetting the sweetness of earth's warm delight,
Forgetting the passionate oneness of love's clasp,
Absolved in the self-rapt immortal's bliss. ||128.11||

Eternal mountains ridge on gleaming ridge
Whose lines were graved as on a sapphire plate
And etched the borders of heaven's lustrous noon
Climbed like piled temple stairs and from their heads
Of topless meditation heard below
The approach of a blue pilgrim multitude
And listened to a great arriving voice
Of the wide travel hymn of timeless seas. ||148.15||

fretted

Above him in a new celestial vault
Other than the heavens beheld by mortal eyes,
As on a fretted ceiling of the gods,
An archipelago of laughter and fire,
Swam stars apart in a rippled sea of sky. ||33.4||

At first her path ran far through peopled tracts:
Admitted to the lion eye of States
And theatres of the loud act of man,
Her carven chariot with its fretted wheels
Threaded through clamorous marts and sentinel towers
Past figured gates and high dream-sculptured fronts
And gardens hung in the sapphire of the skies,
Pillared assembly halls with armoured guards,
Small fanes where one calm Image watched man's life
And temples hewn as if by exiled gods
To imitate their lost eternity. ||99.16||

frescoed

The little ego's ring could join no more;
In the enormous spaces of the self
The body now seemed only a wandering shell,
His mind the many-frescoed outer court
Of an imperishable Inhabitant:
His spirit breathed a superhuman air. ||21.12||

Often from gilded dusk to argent dawn
Where jewel-lamps flickered on frescoed walls
And the stone lattice stared at moonlit boughs,
Half-conscious of the tardy listening night
Dimly she glided between banks of sleep
At rest in the slumbering palaces of kings. ||99.17||

Pranked butterflies, the conscious flowers of air,
The brilliant long bills in their vivid dress,
The peacock scattering on the breeze his moons
Painted my memory like a frescoed wall. ||103.37||

gilded

Often from gilded dusk to argent dawn
Where jewel-lamps flickered on frescoed walls
And the stone lattice stared at moonlit boughs,
Half-conscious of the tardy listening night
Dimly she glided between banks of sleep
At rest in the slumbering palaces of kings.
On these high shining backs falsehood could ride;
Truth lay with delight in error's passionate arms
Gliding downstream in a blithe gilded barge:
She edged her ray with a magnificent lie. ||118.51||

lattice

This brilliant roof of our descending plane,
Intercepting the free boon of heaven's air,
Admits small inrushes of a mighty breath
Or fragrant circuits through gold lattices;
It shields our ceiling of terrestrial mind
From deathless suns and the streaming of God's rain,
Yet canalises a strange irised glow,
And bright dews drip from the Immortal's sky. ||28.9||

Often from gilded dusk to argent dawn
Where jewel-lamps flickered on frescoed walls
And the stone lattice stared at moonlit boughs,
Half-conscious of the tardy listening night
Dimly she glided between banks of sleep
At rest in the slumbering palaces of kings. ||99.17||

limned

There is limned ever retreating from the eyes,
As if in a tenuous misty dream-light drawn,
The outline of a dim mysterious shore. ||17.16||

An opening looked up to spheres above
And coloured shadows limned on mortal ground
The passing figures of immortal things;
A quick celestial flash could sometimes come:
The illumined soul-ray fell on heart and flesh
And touched with semblances of ideal light
The stuff of which our earthly dreams are made. ||44.39||

A magic flowed as if of moving scenes
That kept awhile their fugitive delicacy
Of sparing lines limned by an abstract art
In a rare scanted light with faint dream-brush
On a silver background of incertitude. ||49.9||

As might a soul on Nature's background limned
Stand out for a moment in a house of dream
Created by the ardent breath of life,
So he appeared against the forest verge
Inset twixt green relief and golden ray. ||102.8||

An early child-god took my hand that held,
Moved, guided by the seeking of his touch,
Bright forms and hues which fled across his sight;
Limned upon page and stone they spoke to men. ||103.33||

As might a lightning streak, a glory fell
Nearing until the rapt eyes of the sage
Looked out from luminous cloud and, strangely limned
His face, a beautiful mask of antique joy,
Appearing in light descended where arose
King Aswapathy's palace to the winds
In Madra, flowering up in delicate stone. ||106.14||

All in this world was shadowed forth, not limned,
Like faces leaping on a fan of fire
Or shapes of wonder in a tinted blur,
Like fugitive landscapes painting silver mists. ||139.17||

Its figures are snares that trap and prison the sense;
The beginningless void was its artificer:
Nothing is there but aspects limned by Chance
And seeming shapes of seeming Energy. ||140.91||

The dim-heart marvel of the ideal was lost;
Its crowding wonder of bright delicate dreams
And vague half-limned sublimities she had left:
Thought fell towards lower levels; hard and tense
It passioned for some crude reality. ||143.2||

paint, painters, painting, painted

These unwise prompters of man's ignorant heart
And tutors of his stumbling speech and will,
Movers of petty wraths and lusts and hates
And changeful thoughts and shallow emotion's starts,
These slight illusion-makers with their masks,
Painters of the decor of a dull-hued stage
And nimble scene-shifters of the human play,
Ever are busy with this ill-lit scene. ||45.27||

A hunter of spiritual verities
Still only thought or guessed or held by faith,
It seized in imagination and confined
A painted bird of paradise in a cage. ||50.29||

Overpassing lines that please the outward eyes
But hide the sight of that which lives within
Sculpture and painting concentrated sense
Upon an inner vision's motionless verge,
Revealed a figure of the invisible,
Unveiled all Nature's meaning in a form,
Or caught into a body the Divine. ||95.12||

Pranked butterflies, the conscious flowers of air,
The brilliant long bills in their vivid dress,
The peacock scattering on the breeze his moons
Painted my memory like a frescoed wall. ||103.37||

All seemed a brilliant shadow of itself,
A cosmic film of scenes and images:
The enduring mass and outline of the hills
Was a design sketched on a silent mind
And held to a tremulous false solidity
By constant beats of visionary sight;
The forest with its emerald multitudes
Clothed with its show of hues vague empty Space,
A painting's colours hiding a surface void
That flickered upon dissolution's edge;
The blue heavens, an illusion of the eyes,
Roofed in the mind's illusion of a world. ||130.16||

All in this world was shadowed forth, not limned,
Like faces leaping on a fan of fire
Or shapes of wonder in a tinted blur,
Like fugitive landscapes painting silver mists. ||139.17||

When it would build eternity from the dust,
Man's thought paints images illusion rounds;
Prophesying glories it shall never see,
It labours delicately among its dreams. ||140.14||

How shall the Ideal's unsubstantial hues
Be painted stiff on earth's vermilion blur,
A dream within a dream come doubly true? ||140.120||

O human face, put off mind-painted masks:
The animal be, the worm that Nature meant;
Accept thy futile birth, thy narrow life. ||142.38||

Transient painting on a holiday's floor
Traced for a moment's beauty love was made. ||142.80||

The line above recalls Mary Helen's sudden epiphany when we read Savitri each evening for years and when we worked on the Savitri Lexicon. On reading the lines,

'Transient painting on a holiday's floor'

she said, "Ah, that is a kolam", I had always felt the line should begin with an 'A' but it certainly can read both ways. Actually, this is most often the way Savitri is revealed to us, as revelation, without the intrusion of the mind.

* kolam - In front of every home on special holidays and often even daily, the woman of the house will draw beautiful paintings in chalk on the street. The children too learn this art. It is amazing how quickly the scenes are drawn, using dots placed mathematically, connected and then filled in with brilliant colours.

Look on these forms that stay awhile and pass,
These lives that long and strive, then are no more,
These structures that have no abiding truth,
The saviour creeds that cannot save themselves,
But perish in the strangling hands of the years,
Discarded from man's thought, proved false by Time,
Philosophies that strip all problems bare
But nothing ever have solved since earth began,
And sciences omnipotent in vain
By which men learn of what the suns are made,
Transform all forms to serve their outward needs,
Ride through the sky and sail beneath the sea,
But learn not what they are or why they came;
These polities, architectures of man's brain,

That, bricked with evil and good, wall in man's spirit
And, fissured houses, palace at once and jail,
Rot while they reign and crumble before they crash;
These revolutions, demon or drunken god,
Convulsing the wounded body of mankind
Only to paint in new colours an old face;
These wars, carnage triumphant, ruin gone mad,
The work of centuries vanishing in an hour,
The blood of the vanquished and the victor's crown
Which men to be born must pay for with their pain,
The hero's face divine on satyr's limbs,
The demon's grandeur mixed with the demi-god's,
The glory and the beasthood and the shame;
Why is it all, the labour and the din,
The transient joys, the timeless sea of tears,
The longing and the hoping and the cry,
The battle and the victory and the fall,
The aimless journey that can never pause,
The waking toil, the incoherent sleep? ||144.14||

prints

Oft from her soul stepped out a naked thought
Luminous with mysteried lips and wonderful eyes;
Or from her heart emerged some burning face
And looked for life and love and passionate truth,
Aspired to heaven or embraced the world
Or led the fancy like a fleeting moon
Across the dull sky of man's common days,
Amidst the doubtful certitudes of earth's lore,
To the celestial beauty of faith gave form
As if at flower-prints in a dingy room
Laughed in a golden vase one living rose. ||129.10||

sculptor, sculpture, sculptured

This sculptor of the forms of the Infinite,
This screened unrecognised Inhabitant,
Initiate of his own veiled mysteries,
Hides in a small dumb seed his cosmic thought. ||5.17||

As a sculptor chisels a deity out of stone
He slowly chipped off the dark envelope,
Line of defence of Nature's ignorance,
The illusion and mystery of the Inconscient
In whose black pall the Eternal wraps his head
That he may act unknown in cosmic Time. ||7.21||

But now she turns to break the oblivious spell,
Awakes the sleeper on the sculptured couch;
She finds again the Presence in the form
And in the light that wakes with him recovers
A meaning in the hurry and trudge of Time,
And through this mind that once obscured the soul
Passes a glint of unseen deity. ||50.61||

Overpassing lines that please the outward eyes
But hide the sight of that which lives within
Sculpture and painting concentrated sense
Upon an inner vision's motionless verge,
Revealed a figure of the invisible,
Unveiled all Nature's meaning in a form,
Or caught into a body the Divine. ||95.12||

Escaped from surface sight and mortal sense
The seizing harmony of its shapes became
The strange significant icon of a Power

Renewing its inscrutable descent
Into a human figure of its works
That stood out in life's bold abrupt relief
On the soil of the evolving universe,
A godhead sculptured on a wall of thought,
Mirrored in the flowing hours and dimly shrined
In Matter as in a cathedral cave. ||98.17||

At first her path ran far through peopled tracts:
Admitted to the lion eye of States
And theatres of the loud act of man,
Her carven chariot with its fretted wheels
Threaded through clamorous marts and sentinel towers
Past figured gates and high dream-sculptured fronts
And gardens hung in the sapphire of the skies,
Pillared assembly halls with armoured guards,
Small fanes where one calm Image watched man's life
And temples hewn as if by exiled gods
To imitate their lost eternity. ||99.16||

His instrument the dim corporeal mind,
Of celestial insight now forgetful grown,
He seizes on some sign of outward charm
To guide him mid the throng of Nature's hints,
Reads heavenly truths into earth's semblances,
Desires the image for the Godhead's sake,
Divines the immortalities of form
And takes the body for the sculptured soul. ||102.52||

Pain is the hand of Nature sculpturing men
To greatness: an inspired labour chisels
With heavenly cruelty an unwilling mould. ||108.27||

Flames of self-lost immobile reverie,
Doves crowded the grey musing cornices
Like sculptured postures of white-bosomed peace. ||125.25||

Enigma of the Inconscient's sculptural sleep,
Symbols of the approach to darkness old
And monuments of her titanic reign,
Opening to depths like dumb appalling jaws
That wait a traveller down a haunted path
Attracted to a mystery that slays,
They watched across her road, cruel and still;
Sentinels they stood of dumb Necessity,
Mute heads of vigilant and sullen gloom,
Carved muzzle of a dim enormous world. ||136.24||

Heaven ever young and earth too firm and old
Delay the heart by immobility:
Their raptures of creation last too long,
Their bold formations are too absolute;
Carved by an anguish of divine endeavour
They stand up sculptured on the eternal hills,
Or quarried from the living rocks of God
Win immortality by perfect form. ||139.13||

On a brink held of senseless ecstasy
And guarding an eternal poise of thought
Sat sculptured souls dreaming by rivers of sound
In changeless attitudes of marble bliss. ||148.17||

sketch, sketched

This faint and fluid sketch of soul called man
Shall stand out on the background of long Time
A glowing epitome of eternity,
A little point reveal the infinitudes. ||26.25||

Our vague beginnings are overtaken there,
Our middle terms sketched out in prescient lines,
Our finished ends anticipated live. ||28.8||

Yet was this only a provisional scheme,
A false appearance sketched by limiting sense,
Mind's insufficient self-discovery,
An early attempt, a first experiment. ||47.1||

The mighty Mother's whims and lightning moods
Arisen from her all-wise unruled delight
In the freedom of her sweet and passionate breast,
Robbed of their wonder were chained to a cause and aim;
An idol of bronze replaced her mystic shape
That captures the movements of the cosmic vasts,
In the sketch precise of an ideal face
Forgotten was her eyelashes' dream-print
Carrying on their curve infinity's dreams,
Lost the alluring marvel of her eyes;
The surging wave-throbs of her vast sea-heart
They bound to a theorem of ordered beats:
Her deep designs which from herself she had veiled
Bowed self-revealed in their confessional. ||71.37||

The tree of evolution I have sketched,
Each branch and twig and leaf in its own place,
In the embryo tracked the history of forms,
And the genealogy framed of all that lives. ||71.37||

This mind is a dynamic small machine
Producing ceaselessly till it wears out,
With raw material drawn from the outside world,
The patterns sketched out by an artist God. ||129.29||

All seemed a brilliant shadow of itself,
A cosmic film of scenes and images:
The enduring mass and outline of the hills
Was a design sketched on a silent mind
And held to a tremulous false solidity

By constant beats of visionary sight;
The forest with its emerald multitudes
Clothed with its show of hues vague empty Space,
A painting's colours hiding a surface void
That flickered upon dissolution's edge;
The blue heavens, an illusion of the eyes,
Roofed in the mind's illusion of a world. ||130.16||

statue, statuettes

A Presence wrought behind the ambiguous screen:
It beat his soil to bear a Titan's weight,
Refining half-hewn blocks of natural strength
It built his soul into a statued God. ||5.31||

On a commissioned keel his merchant hull
Serves the world's commerce in the riches of Time
Severing the foam of a great land-locked sea
To reach unknown harbour lights in distant climes
And open markets for life's opulent arts,
Rich bales, carved statuettes, hued canvases,
And jewelled toys brought for an infant's play
And perishable products of hard toil
And transient splendours won and lost by the days. ||17.7||

Here even the highest rapture Time can give
Is a mimicry of ungrasped beatitudes,
A mutilated statue of ecstasy,
A wounded happiness that cannot live,
A brief felicity of mind or sense
Thrown by the World-Power to her body-slave,
Or a simulacrum of enforced delight
In the seraglios of Ignorance. ||19.14||

This solid mass which brooked no throb of sense
Could not contain their vast creative urge:

Immersed no more in Matter's harmony,
The Spirit lost its statuesque repose. ||36.10||

A mastering virtue statuesques the pose,
Or a titan passion goads to a proud unrest:
At Wisdom's altar they are kings and priests
Or their life a sacrifice to an idol of Power. ||51.24||

On the dark background of a soulless world
She staged between a lurid light and shade
Her dramas of the sorrow of the depths
Written on the agonised nerves of living things:
Epics of horror and grim majesty,
Wry statues spat and stiffened in life's mud,
A glut of hideous forms and hideous deeds
Paralysed pity in the hardened breast. ||58.10||

In the magnificent dawning of his force
Built like a moving statue of delight
He illumined the border of the forest page. ||102.12||

As if self-poised above the march of days,
Her immobile spirit watched the haste of Time,
A statue of passion and invincible force,
An absolutism of sweet imperious will,
A tranquillity and a violence of the gods
Indomitable and immutable. ||114.19||

As the Voice touched, her body became a stark
And rigid golden statue of motionless trance,
A stone of God lit by an amethyst soul. ||116.4||

Then Savitri by her doomed husband sat,
Still rigid in her golden motionless pose,
A statue of the fire of the inner sun. ||116.27||

Still like a statue on its pedestal,
Lone in the silence and to vastness bared,
Against midnight's dumb abysses piled in front
A columned shaft of fire and light she rose. ||136.38||

My first strong grief moves not my seated mind;
My unwept tears have turned to pearls of strength:
I have transformed my ill-shaped brittle clay
Into the hardness of a statued soul. ||137.58||

It has no voice to answer to his call,
No feet that move, no hands to take his gifts:
Aerial statue of the nude Idea,
Virgin conception of a bodiless god,
Its light stirs man the thinker to create
An earthly semblance of diviner things. ||140.21||

Ascetic voices called of lonely seers
On mountain summits or on river banks
Or from the desolate heart of forest glades
Seeking heaven's rest or the spirit's worldless peace,
Or in bodies motionless like statues, fixed
In tranced cessations of their sleepless thought
Sat sleeping souls, and this too was a dream. ||143.13||

My adoration mastered, my desire
Bent down to make its subject, my daring clasped,
Claiming by body and soul my life's estate,
Rapture's possession, love's sweet property,
A statue of silence in my templed spirit,
A yearning godhead and a golden bride. ||157.29||

Dictionary

When a disciple from India needed clarification of certain words the Lexicon was enlarged, understanding that for many whose first language is not English there are numerous words with multiple definitions, many so profound as to be puzzling or seemingly obscure, or not readily accessible to being defined. For this reason we revisited the entire text and began to include words that may be felt by some familiar with English to be "common" yet are employed by Sri Aurobindo in unique ways in Savitri. For the series, Inspiration from Savitri, it was necessary to exclude many words that are defined in the Lexicon to prevent them fro becoming unwieldy.

abhorred Regarded with extreme repugnance, aversion or disgust; detested; loathed. **abhorring.**

abide 1. To wait, stay, remain. **2.** To remain in residence; to sojourn, reside, dwell. **3.** To remain with; to stand firm by, to hold to, remain true to. **4.** To continue in existence, endure, stand firm or sure. **abides, abode, abiding.**

abrupt 1. Characterized by sudden interruption or change; unannounced and unexpected; sudden, hasty. **2.** Precipitous, steep. **3.** Of strata: Suddenly cropping out and presenting their edges.

absolutism An absolute standard or principle.

abyss 1. The great deep, the primal chaos; the 'bowels of the earth', the supposed cavity of the lower world; the 'infernal pit'. **2.** A bottomless gulf; any unfathomable or apparently unfathomable cavity or void space; a profound gulf, chasm, or void extending beneath. **Abyss, abyss's, abysses.**

accustomed 1. Customary, habitual, usual. **2.** Habituated; acclimated (usually followed by *to*).

acolyte An attendant or junior assistant in any ceremony or operation; a novice; follower. **acolytes.**

adept One who is completely versed (in something); thoroughly proficient; well-skilled; expert. **adepts.**

adjunct Joined or added (to anything); connected, annexed; subordinate in position, function, character, or essence. **adjuncts.**

adversary A person, group or force that opposes or attacks, or acts in a hostile manner; an opponent, antagonist; an enemy, foe. **adversary's.**

Adversary.

Sri Aurobindo: "When there is some lowering or diminution of the consciousness or some impairing of it at one place or another, the Adversary -- or the Censor -- who is always on the watch presses with all his might wherever there is a weak point lying covered from your own view, and suddenly a wrong movement leaps up with unexpected force. Become conscious and cast out the possibility of its renewal, that is all that is to be done." *Letters on Yoga*

The Mother: "To conquer the Adversary is not a small thing. One must have a greater power than his to vanquish him. But one can liberate oneself totally from his influence. And from the minute one is completely free from his influence, one's self-giving can be total. And with the self-giving comes joy, long before the Adversary is truly vanquished and disappears."

"The Adversary will disappear only when he is no longer necessary in the world. And we know very well that he is necessary, as the touch-stone for gold: to know if it is pure. But if one is really sincere, the Adversary can't even approach him any longer; and he doesn't try it, because that would be courting his own destruction." *Questions and Answers 1955, MCW Vol. 7.*

" . . . insincerity is always an open door for the adversary. That means there is some secret sympathy with what is perverse. And that is what is serious." *Questions and Answers 1957-58, MCW Vol. 9.*

adytum The innermost part of a temple; the secret shrine whence oracles were delivered; a most sacred or reserved part of any place of worship; hence, *fig.* a private or inner chamber, a sanctum.

aesthesis The perception of the external world by the senses.

Sri Aurobindo: "By aesthesis is meant a reaction of the consciousness, mental and vital and even bodily, which receives a certain element in things, something that can be called their taste, Rasa, which, passing through the mind or sense or both, awakes a vital enjoyment of the taste, Bhoga, and this can again awaken us, awaken even the soul in us to something yet deeper and more fundamental than mere pleasure and enjoyment, to some form of the spirit's delight of existence, Ananda." *Letters on Savitri*

"Aesthesis therefore is of the very essence of poetry, as it is of all art. But it is not the sole element and aesthesis too is not confined to a reception of poetry and art; it extends to everything in the world: there is nothing we can sense, think or in any way experience to which there cannot be an aesthetic reaction of our conscious being. Ordinarily, we suppose that aesthesis is concerned with beauty, and that indeed is its most prominent concern: but it is concerned with many other things also. It is the universal Ananda that is the parent of aesthesis and the universal Ananda takes three major and original forms, beauty, love and delight, the delight of all existence, the delight in things, in all things." *Letters on Savitri*

"This universal aesthesis of beauty and delight does not ignore or fail to understand the differences and oppositions, the gradations, the harmony and disharmony obvious to the ordinary consciousness; but, first of all, it draws a Rasa from them and with that comes the enjoyment, Bhoga. and the touch or the mass of the Ananda. It sees that all things have their meaning, their value, their deeper or total significance which the mind does not see, for the mind is only concerned with a surface vision, surface contacts and its own surface reactions. When something expresses perfectly what it was meant to express, the completeness brings with it a sense of harmony, a sense of artistic perfection; it gives even to what is discordant a place in a system of cosmic concordances and the discords become part of a vast harmony, and wherever there is harmony, there is a sense of beauty. " *Letters on Savitri*

affranchised Freed from a state of dependence, servitude or obligation;

alcoves Recessed spaces, as bowers in a garden; arched recesses or niches in the wall of any structure.

altar **1.** A block, pile, table, stand, mound, platform, or other elevated structure on which to place or sacrifice offerings to a deity. **2.** With reference to the uses, customs, dedication, or peculiar sanctity of the altar. **3.** A place consecrated to devotional observances. **altar's, altars, altar-burnings, mountain-altars.**

Anarchs Authors or advocates of anarchy; leaders of revolt.

anarchy A state of society without government or law ; lawlessness, confusion, chaos, disorder.

anchorites Those who have retired to a solitary place for a life of religious seclusion; hermits, recluses.

annexed Attached appended, or added.

annul **1.** To reduce to nothing; obliterate; annihilate. To put out of existence, extinguish. **2.** To put an end or stop to (an action or state of things); to abolish, cancel, do away with. **3.** To make void or null; abolish; cancel; invalidate; declare invalid. **annuls, annulled, annulling, annulment.**

antre A cavern; cave. **antres.**

appalled Filled or overcome with horror, consternation, or fear, resulting in the loss of courage in the face of something dreadful.

appalling Causing dismay or horror; shocking.

apparelled Adorned; covered; decorated; clothed. **apparels.**

Apsaras   Sri Aurobindo: "The Apsaras are the most beautiful and romantic conception on the lesser plane of Hindu mythology. From the moment that they arose out of the waters of the milky Ocean, robed in ethereal raiment and heavenly adornment, waking melody from a million lyres, the beauty and light of them has transformed the world. They crowd in the sunbeams, they flash and gleam over heaven in the lightnings, they make the azure beauty of the sky; they are the light of sunrise and sunset and the haunting voices of forest and field. They dwell too in the life of the soul; for they are the ideal pursued by the poet through his lines, by the artist shaping his soul on his canvas, by the sculptor seeking a form in the marble; for the joy of their embrace the hero flings his life into the rushing torrent of battle; the sage, musing upon God, sees the shining of their limbs and falls from his white ideal. The delight of life, the beauty of things, the attraction of sensuous beauty, this is what the mystic and romantic side of the Hindu temperament strove to express in the Apsara. The original meaning is everywhere felt as a shining background, but most in the older allegories, especially the strange and romantic legend of Pururavas as we first have it in the Brahmanas and the Vishnoupurana.

The Apsaras then are the divine Hetairae of Paradise, beautiful singers and actresses whose beauty and art relieve the arduous and world-long struggle of the Gods against the forces that tend towards disruption by the Titans who would restore Matter to its original atomic condition or of dissolution by the sages and hermits who would make phenomena dissolve prematurely into the One who is above phenomena. They rose from the Ocean, says Valmiki, seeking who should choose them as brides, but neither the Gods nor the Titans accepted them, therefore are they said to be common or universal. *The Harmony of Virtue*

apse   A usually semicircular or polygonal, often vaulted recess, especially the termination of the sanctuary end of a church.

apt   **1.** Having a natural tendency; inclined; disposed. **2.** Unusually intelligent; able to learn quickly and easily. **3.** Exactly suitable; appropriate.

arabesques   **1.** Any ornaments or ornamental objects such as rugs or mosaics, in which flowers, foliage, fruits, vases, animals, and figures are represented in a fancifully combined pattern. **2.** *Fine Arts.* A sinuous, spiraling, undulating, or serpentine line or linear motif.

arc-lamps General term for a class of lamps in which light is produced by a voltaic arc, a luminous arc between two electrodes typically made of tungsten or carbon and barely separated.

arch-mason *Fig.* Master builder. **Archmason, archmasons.**

archipelago 1. Any sea, or body of water, in which there are numerous islands. **2.** A large group or chain of islands.

ardent 1. Having, expressive of, or characterized by intense feeling; glowing with passion, animated by keen desire; intensely eager, zealous, fervent, fervid. **2.** Burning, fiery, or hot. **ardent-hued.**

argent Resembling silver; silvery white.

arrested Stopped, checked the course of, stayed, slowed down. **arresting.**

artifice 1. An artful or crafty expedient; a stratagem. **2.** Cleverness or skill; ingenuity; inventiveness.

artificer 1. One who is skilful or clever in devising ways of making things; inventor. **2.** A skilful or artistic worker; craftsperson. **artificers.**

artisan One skilled in an applied art; craftsperson. **artisans.**

ascetic One who dedicates his or her life to a pursuit of contemplative ideals, whether by seclusion or by abstinence from creature comforts, and practices extreme self-denial, rigorous self-discipline or self-mortification. **ascetic's, ascetics.**

aspirant *n.* **1.** One who seeks with eagerness and steady purpose. *adj.* **2.** Aspiring, striving for a higher position; mounting up, ascending. **aspirants.**

assail 1. To attack vigorously or violently; assault. **2.** To impinge upon; make an impact on; beset. **3.** To take upon oneself a difficult challenge with the intention of mastering it. **assailed, assailing.**

assent **1.** Agreement, as to a proposal; concurrence. **2.** Acquiescence; compliance, concession. **assents, assenting.**

assessed Evaluated (a person or thing); estimated (the quality, value, or extent of), gauged or judged.

assigned Appointed, designated, deputed, allotted, announced as a task. **assigner.**

assume **1.** To take upon oneself, to adopt an aspect, form, or attribute. **2.** To take on titles, offices, duties, responsibilities. **3.** To take on as one's own, to adopt. **assumes, assumed, assuming.**

Aswapati Sri Aurobindo: "Aswapati, the Lord of the Horse, her [Savitri's] human father, is the Lord of Tapasya, the concentrated energy of spiritual endeavour that helps us to rise from the mortal to the immortal planes; . . . ." (From a letter written by Sri Aurobindo) **Aswapati's.**

audacious **1.** Spirited and original; daring; bold. **2.** Fearlessly, often recklessly daring; bold; defiant; insolent; brazen; unrestrained by convention or propriety.

aureate Golden or gilded; brilliant or splendid.

austere **1.** Severe in manner or appearance; uncompromising; strict; forbidding; stark. **2.** Rigorously self-disciplined and severely moral; ascetic; abstinent. **3.** Grave; sober; solemn; serious. **4.** Without excess, luxury, or ease; severely simple; without ornament. **austerity.**

awed **1.** inspired or influenced by a feeling of fearful wonderment or reverence; **2.** Inspired with reverential wonder combined with an element of latent fear.

babel "The reference is to the mythological story of the construction of the Tower of Babel, which appears to be an attempt to explain the diversity of human languages. According to Genesis, the Babylonians wanted to make a name for themselves by building a mighty city and tower 'with its top in the heavens'. God disrupted the work by so confusing the language of the workers that they could no longer understand one another. The tower was never completed and the people were dispersed over the face of the earth." *(Encyclopaedia Britannica) Glossary and Index of Proper Names in Sri Aurobindo's Works*

Sri Aurobindo: "The legend of the Tower of Babel speaks of the diversity of tongues as a curse laid on the race; but whatever its disadvantages, and they tend more and more to be minimised by the growth of civilisation and increasing intercourse, it has been rather a blessing than a curse, a gift to mankind rather than a disability laid upon it. The purposeless exaggeration of anything is always an evil, and an excessive pullulation of varying tongues that serve no purpose in the expression of a real diversity of spirit and culture is certainly a stumbling-block rather than a help: but this excess, though it existed in the past, is hardly a possibility of the future. The tendency is rather in the opposite direction. In former times diversity of language helped to create a barrier to knowledge and sympathy, was often made the pretext even of an actual antipathy and tended to a too rigid division. The lack of sufficient interpenetration kept up both a passive want of understanding and a fruitful crop of active misunderstandings. But this was an inevitable evil of a particular stage of growth, an exaggeration of the necessity that then existed for the vigorous development of strongly individualised group-souls in the human race. These disadvantages have not yet been abolished, but with closer intercourse and the growing desire of men and nations for the knowledge of each other's thought and spirit and personality, they have diminished and tend to diminish more and more and there is no reason why in the end they should not become inoperative." *The Human Cycle*

Babel-builders'.

bacchant *n.* **1.** A priest or votary of Bacchus (the god of wine). **2.** A drunken reveller. *adj.* **3.** Inclined to revelry. **Bacchant.**

bacchic Of or relating to Bacchus; drunken and carousing; riotously intoxicated.

bards An ancient Celtic order of minstrel poets who composed and recited verses celebrating the legendary exploits of chieftains and heroes. **2.** Poets, especially lyric poets.

barrage An overwhelming quantity or explosion as of artillery fire, words, blows, or criticisms.

basilicas Public buildings in ancient Rome having a central nave with an apse at one or both ends and two side aisles formed by rows of columns, which was used as an assembly hall – also Christian churches with a similar design.

beam **1.** A ray of light. **2.** A ray or collection of parallel rays. **3.** A column of light, a gleam, emanation. Also *fig.* **beams.**

beasthood The state or nature of a beast.

beatitude Supreme blessedness or happiness. **beatitude's, beatitudes.**

behest An authoritative command or directive.

besiege **1.** To surround with hostile forces. **2.** To crowd around; hem in; crowd in upon; surround. **besieged**

blinkered Subjective and limited, as in viewpoint or perception.

blockade **1.** The isolating, closing off, or surrounding of a place. **2.** Any obstruction of passage or progress.

bough A main branch on a tree. **boughs.**

bower A shaded, leafy recess; an arbour; also *poetic,* an abode.

breadth **1.** The measure or the second largest dimension of a plane or solid figure; width. **2.** Freedom from narrowness or restraint; liberality. **3.** Tolerance; broadmindedness. **breadths.**

brooding **1.** *Fig.* Protecting (young) by or as if by covering with the wings. **2.** Meditating or dwelling deeply on a thought.

brook To put up with, tolerate. **brooked**

buffer state A nation lying between potentially hostile larger nations.

calculus A method of calculation, *esp.* one of several highly systematic methods of treating problems by a special system of algebraic notations, as differential or integral calculus.

camest A native English form of the verb, *to come*, now only in formal and poetic usage.

canalise To divert into certain channels; give a certain direction to or provide a certain outlet for, in order to control or regulate. **canalises, canalised.**

caprice 1. A sudden, unpredictable change or series of actions or changes. **2.** A sudden, unpredictable change, as of one's mind; whim, fancy. **caprices.**

caricature A grotesque imitation, misrepresentation or distorted image, as a drawing or description of a person which exaggerates characteristic features for comic effect.

carnage Massive slaughter, as in war; a massacre.

casements Window sashes that open outward by means of hinges.

cast *v.* **1.** To throw with force; hurl. **2.** To form (liquid metal, for example) into a particular shape by pouring into a mould. Also *fig.* **3.** To cause to fall upon something or in a certain direction; send forth. **4.** To throw on the ground, as in wrestling. **5.** To put or place, *esp.* hastily or forcibly. **6.** To direct (the eye, a glance, etc.) **7.** To throw (something) forth or off. **8.** To bestow; confer. **casts, casting.**

cathedral 1. A large and important church of imposing architectural beauty. **2.** Of, relating to, or resembling a cathedral.

causeway 1. A raised roadway, as across water or marshland. **2.** A paved highway.

cavern A large underground chamber, as in a cave. **caverns, cavern-passages.**

celestial 1. Of or relating to the sky or the heavens. **2.** Of or relating to heaven; divine. **3.** Heavenly; divine; spiritual. **celestials', celestial-human.**

Centaur *Greek Mythology*, one of a race of monsters having the head, arms, and trunk of a man and the body and legs of a horse. **centaur's, Centaur, Centaur's.**

"A fabulous tribe of wild, beastlike monsters, having the upper part of a human being and the lower part of a horse. They live in the woods or mountains of Elis, Arcadia, and Thessaly. They are representative of wild life, animal desires and barbarism. (M.I.) *Glossary and Index of Proper Names in Sri Aurobindo's Works.*

chant *n.* **1.** A short, simple series of syllables or words that are sung on or intoned to the same note or a limited range of notes. **2.** A song or melody. *v.* **3.** To sing, especially in the manner of a chant. **chants, chanted, chanting, chantings.**

chaos **1.** The infinity of space or formless matter supposed to have preceded the existence of the ordered universe. **2.** A condition, place, or state of great disorder or confusion. **3.** A disorderly mass; a jumble. **Chaos.**

chapel A place of worship that is smaller than and subordinate to a church.

charade A game in which each syllable of a word, and then the whole word, is acted and the audience has to guess the word.

chattel A slave.

chiaroscuro **1.** The arrangement of light and dark elements in a pictorial work of art. **2.** *Poetic*: Contrasting sense as in, darkness and light, 'joy and gloom', 'praise and blame,' etc.

chrysolites Brown or yellow-green olivine found in igneous and metamorphic rocks and used as gemstones such as topaz, etc.

cipher *n.* **1.** Something having no influence or value; a zero; a nonentity. **2.** A secret method of writing, as by transposition or substitution of letters, specially formed symbols, or the like. unintelligible to all but those possessing the key; a cryptograph. **ciphers.** *v.* **3.** To put in secret writing; encode. **ciphers.** Note: Sri Aurobindo also spelled the word as Cypher, the old English spelling.

Circean Relating to or resembling Circe, the fabled enchantress described by Homer. She was supposed to possess great knowledge of magic and venomous herbs which she offered as a drink to her charmed and fascinated victims who then changed into swine; hence, pleasing, but harmful; fascinating, but degrading.

citadel A fortress that commands a city and is used in the control of the inhabitants and in defence during attack or siege. **citadels.**

clamant Clamorous; loud; noisy.

clamorous 1. Full of, marked by, or of the nature of clamour; shouting; noisy, loud. **2.** Insistently demanding attention; importunate.

clang 1. A loud resounding noise, as a large bell or metal when struck. **2.** *v.* To make or cause to make, or produce a loud ringing, resonant sound as of a large bell.

cleft 1. A crack, crevice, or split. **2.** A long narrow opening. **clefts.**

clipped Cut off; curtailed; diminished.

cloistering Shutting away from the world in or as if in a cloister; secluding.

cloved

coeval 1. Of the same era, period or age. **2.** A contemporary.

coin 1. A small piece of metal, usually flat and circular, authorized by a government for use as money. **2.** A mode of expression considered standard, a symbol; token.

colonnade ('s) A series of columns placed at regular intervals.

companioning Accompanying someone or being a companion to.

compendium 1. A brief treatment or account of a subject, *esp.* an extensive subject; concise treatise. **2.** A short, complete summary; an abstract.

conceive 1. To form or hold an idea. **2.** To begin, originate, or found (something) in a particular way (usually used in the passive). **3.** To apprehend mentally; understand. **4.** To be created or formed in the womb; to be engendered; begotten. **conceives, conceived, self-conceived.**

concupiscence Strong desire, especially sexual desire; lust.

confessional A small enclosed stall in which a priest hears confessions.

conjecture The formation of conclusions from incomplete evidence; guess. **conjecture's, world-conjecture's.**

consequence 1. Something that logically or naturally follows from an action or condition. **2.** Significance; importance.

Sri Aurobindo: " Karma is nothing but the will of the Spirit in action, consequence nothing but the creation of will. What is in the will of being, expresses itself in karma and consequence. When the will is limited in mind, karma appears as a bondage and a limitation, consequence as a reaction or an imposition. But when the will of the being is infinite in the spirit, karma and consequence become instead the joy of the creative spirit, the construction of the eternal mechanist, the word and drama of the eternal poet, the harmony of the eternal musician, the play of the eternal child." *Essays in Philosophy and Yoga*

consort *n.* **1.** A companion or partner. **consort's.** *v.* **2.** To keep company; associate. **consorts.**

contrivance 1. The act or faculty of devising or adapting; inventive skill or ability *esp.* in a negative sense. **2.** The act or manner of contriving; the faculty or power of contriving. inventing or making with thought and skill; invention.

convicting That which points out or impresses upon something its error.

convulsing Shaking violently; agitating physically.

cornices Prominent, continuous, horizontally projecting features surmounting a wall or other construction, or dividing it horizontally for compositional purposes; i.e. to crown or complete a building.

corporeal Of, relating to, or characteristic of the body.

cosmic Of or pertaining to the cosmos and characteristic of its phenomena as forming a part of the material universe; infinite.

Sri Aurobindo: "There is no difference between the terms 'universal' and 'cosmic' except that 'universal' can be used in a freer way than 'cosmic'. Universal may mean 'of the universe', cosmic in that general sense. But it may also mean 'common to all', e.g., 'This is a universal weakness' -- but you cannot say 'This is a cosmic weakness'." *Letters on Yoga*

cosmic Will Sri Aurobindo: "Agni is the Deva, the All-Seer, manifested as conscious-force or, as it would be called in modern language, Divine or Cosmic Will, first hidden and building up the eternal worlds, then manifest, ``born'', building up in man the Truth and the Immortality." *The Secret of the Veda*

Sri Aurobindo: "There is no necessity in the essential nature of mind, sense, life that they should be so limited: for the physical sense-organs are not the creators of sense-perceptions, but themselves the creation, the instruments and here a necessary convenience of the cosmic sense; the nervous system and vital organs are not the creators of life's action and reaction, but themselves the creation, the instruments and here a necessary convenience of the cosmic Life-force; the brain is not the creator of thought, but itself the creation, the instrument and here a necessary convenience of the cosmic Mind. The necessity then is not absolute, but teleological; it is the result of a divine cosmic Will in the material universe which intends to posit here a physical relation between sense and its object, establishes here a material formula and law of Conscious-Force and creates by it physical images of Conscious-Being to serve as the initial, dominating and determining fact of the world in which we live. It is not a fundamental law of being, but a constructive principle necessitated by the intention of the Spirit to evolve in a world of Matter." *The Life Divine*

"Moreover we see that this cosmic action or any cosmic action is impossible without the play of an infinite Force of Existence which produces and regulates all these forms and movements; and that Force equally presupposes or is the action of an infinite Consciousness, because it is in its nature a cosmic Will determining all relations and apprehending them by its own mode of awareness, and it could not so determine and apprehend them if there were no comprehensive

Consciousness behind that mode of cosmic awareness to originate as well as to hold, fix and reflect through it the relations of Being in the developing formation or becoming of itself which we call a universe." *The Life Divine*

"It is not possible for the individual mind, so long as it remains shut up in its personality, to understand the workings of the Cosmic Will, for the standards made by the personal consciousness are not applicable to them. A cell in the body, if conscious, might also think that the human being and its actions are only the resultant of the relations and workings of a number of cells like itself and not the action of a unified self. It is only if one enters into the Cosmic Consciousness that one begins to see the forces at work and the lines on which they work and get a glimpse of the Cosmic Self and the Cosmic Mind and Will." *Letters on Yoga*

"The Cosmic Will is not, to our ordinary consciousness, something that acts as an independent power doing whatever it chooses; it works through all these beings, through the forces at play in the world and the law of these forces and their results -- it is only when we open ourselves and get out of the ordinary consciousness that we can feel it intervening as an independent power and overriding the ordinary play of the forces." *Letters on Yoga*

"Then too we can see that even in the play of the forces and in spite of their distortions the Cosmic Will is working towards the eventual realisation of the Will of the Transcendent Divine." *Letters on Yoga*

"A cosmic Will and Wisdom observant of the ascending march of the soul's consciousness and experience as it emerges out of subconscient Matter and climbs to its own luminous divinity fixes the norm and constantly enlarges the lines of the law -- or, let us say, since law is a too mechanical conception, -- the truth of Karma." *Essays in Philosophy and Yoga*

"Everything here is not perfect but all works out the cosmic Will in the course of the ages." *Letters on Yoga.*

cosmicity ('s) A word coined by Sri Aurobindo. The suffix *ity* is used to form abstract nouns expressing state or condition. Hence, cosmicity refers to a cosmic state or condition.

couchant 1. Lying down; crouching, with the head raised. **2.** (Of an animal) Lying on the stomach with head raised and legs pointed forward.

covert 1. Secret or hidden from view or knowledge; not openly practiced or engaged in, shown or avowed. **2.** Concealment; secrecy. **3.** A covered place or shelter; hiding place.

cowled Wearing or supplied with a cowl; hooded. **self-cowled.**

crabbed 1. Difficult to understand; complicated; obscure. **2.** Difficult to read; cramped; as crabbed handwriting.

Creatrix The Divine Mother, the creatress. **creatrix.** (Sri Aurobindo also employs the word as an *adj.*)

Sri Aurobindo:

**"O Wisdom-Splendour, Mother of the universe,
Creatrix, the Eternal's artist Bride,"** *Savitri*

creed 1. A formal statement of religious belief; a confession of faith. **2.** Any system or codification of belief or of opinion. **creeds.**

crevices Narrow cracks or openings; fissures or clefts.

cricket Any of several jumping insects with long antennae, known for their squeaking and chirping sounds. **crickets'.**

crude 1. In a raw or unprepared state; unrefined or natural; unfinished, coarse. **2.** Lacking in intellectual subtlety, perceptivity, etc.; rudimentary; undeveloped. **3.** Rough or primitive. **4.** Lacking culture, refinement, tact. **crudely.**

crypt 1. An underground vault or chamber, especially one beneath a church that is used as a burial place. **2.** A cellar, vault or tunnel. **3.** *A* location for secret meetings, etc. **crypts.**

cryptic 1. Secret; occult. **2.** Mysterious in meaning; puzzling; ambiguous.

cult 1. Obsessive, especially faddish, devotion to or veneration for a person, principle, or thing. **2.** A specific system of religious worship, *esp.* with reference to its rites and deity. **3.** A group or sect bound together by veneration of the same thing, person, ideal. **cults.**

Cyclopean Pertaining to one of a race of giants having a single eye in the middle of the forehead or any of three one-eyed Titans who forged thunderbolts for Zeus.

daedal *n.* **1.** Complex or intricate. *adj.* **2.** Skilful or ingenious.

daemonic One's indwelling spirit, or genius.

decree *n.* **1.** A formal and authoritative order, *esp.* one having the force of law. **2.** A judicial decision or order. **3.** *Theol.* One of the eternal purposes of God by which events are foreordained. *v.* **4.** To command, ordain, decide by decree. **Decree, decrees, decreed, decreeing.**

deified **1.** Made a god of; exalted to the rank of a deity. **2.** Regarded or adored as a deity.

deliver **1.** To give into another's possession or keeping; surrender. **2.** To set free or liberate; emancipate, release. **3.** To rescue or save. **4.** To assist (a female) in bringing forth young. **5.** To disburden (oneself) of thoughts, opinions, etc. **delivered, delivering, deliverers.**

demigod A mythological being who is partly divine and partly human; an inferior deity. **demigod's, demigods.**

demon An evil spirit; devil or fiend. **demon's, demons.**

Sri Aurobindo: "The typal worlds do not change. In his own world a god is always a god, the Asura always an Asura, the demon always a demon. To change they must either migrate into an evolutionary body or else die entirely to themselves that they may be new born into other Nature." *Essays Divine and Human*

demon Sign demoniac *v.* **1.** Possessed, produced, or influenced by a demon. **2.** Of, resembling, or suggestive of a devil; fiendish. *n.* **3.** One who is or seems to be possessed by a demon.

denizens Inhabitants; occupants; residents, especially of plants or animals and people established in a place to which they are not native.

dependencies Subject territories that are not an integral part of the ruling country.

device   **1.** Something devised or framed by art or inventive power; an invention, contrivance for some particular purpose. **2.** A plan or scheme, especially a malign one. **3.** Something elaborately or fancifully designed. **devices.**

dialect   **1.** The manner or style of expressing oneself in language. **2.** A form of a language that is considered inferior.

diligent   Quietly and steadily persevering especially in detail or exactness while serving others.

din   A jumble of loud, usually discordant sounds.

Dionysian   **1.** Of or relating Dionysus, the Greek god of wine, fruitfulness, and vegetation, worshipped in orgiastic rites and festivals in his name. He was also known as the bestower of ecstasy and god of the drama, and identified with Bacchus. **2.** Recklessly uninhibited; unrestrained.

dire   **1.** Causing or involving great fear or suffering; dreadful; terrible. **2.** Indicating trouble, disaster, misfortune, or the like. **3.** Urgent; desperate. **direr.**

disharmonising   Causing to sound harsh and unpleasant; making discordant or disharmonious.

disquieting   Causing anxiety or uneasiness; disturbing.

divulged   Made known (something private or secret).

Djinn   (Islam) an invisible spirit mentioned in the Koran and believed by Muslims to inhabit the earth and influence mankind by appearing in the form of humans or animals. **djinns .**

dolorous   Full of, expressing, or causing pain or sorrow; grievous; mournful. **dolorously.**

don   To put on or dress in. **dons, donned, donning.**

dread   *n.* **1.** Profound fear; terror. **2.** An object of fear, awe, or reverence. *v.* **3.** To be in fear or terror of. **4.** To anticipate with alarm, distaste, or reluctance. *adj.* **5.** Fearful terrible; causing terror. **6.** Held in awe or reverential fear. **Dread, dreads, dreaded.**

drove A large mass of people moving or acting as a body. (Also *pt.* of **drive.**)

dubious **1.** Marked by or causing doubt; vague; ambiguous. **2.** Not certain in outcome. **3.** Fraught with uncertainty or doubt; undecided.

dullard A person regarded as mentally dull; a dolt.

dumb **1.** Lacking the power of speech. **2.** Producing no sound; silent; mute. **dumbness.**

earthiness *Fig.* Grossly material, coarse, dull, unrefined.

ecstasy **1.** Intense joy or delight. **2.** A state of exalted emotion so intense that one is carried beyond thought. **3.** Used by mystical writers as the technical name for the state of rapture in which the body was supposed to become incapable of sensation, while the soul was engaged in the contemplation of divine things. **4.** The trance, frenzy, or rapture associated with mystic or prophetic exaltation. **Ecstasy, ecstasy's, ecstasies, ecstasied, self-ecstasy, strange-ecstasied.**

"Sri Aurobindo: "It has been held that ecstasy is a lower and transient passage, the peace of the Supreme is the supreme realisation, the consummate abiding experience. This may be true on the spiritual-mind plane: there the first ecstasy felt is indeed a spiritual rapture, but it can be and is very usually mingled with a supreme happiness of the vital parts taken up by the Spirit; there is an exaltation, exultation, excitement, a highest intensity of the joy of the heart and the pure inner soul-sensation that can be a splendid passage or an uplifting force but is not the ultimate permanent foundation. But in the highest ascents of the spiritual bliss there is not this vehement exaltation and excitement; there is instead an illimitable intensity of participation in an eternal ecstasy which is founded on the eternal Existence and therefore on a beatific tranquillity of eternal peace. Peace and ecstasy cease to be different and become one. The Supermind, reconciling and fusing all differences as well as all contradictions, brings out this unity; a wide calm and a deep delight of all-existence are among its first steps of self-realisation, but this calm and this delight rise together, as one state, into an increasing intensity and culminate in the eternal ecstasy, the bliss that is the Infinite." *The Life Divine*

eddy **1.** A current at variance with the main current in a stream of liquid or gas, *esp.* one having a rotary or whirling motion. **2.** A small whirlpool. **eddies, eddying.**

efface **1.** To wipe out; do away with; expunge. **2.** To rub out, erase, or obliterate (outlines, traces, inscriptions, etc.). **3.** To make (oneself) inconspicuous; withdraw (oneself). **effaced, effacing.**

Eldorado(s) **1.** A legendary treasure city of South America believed to contain an abundance of gold, sought by the early Spanish Conquistadors. **2.** Any place offering great wealth.

Elysian Of the nature of, or resembling, what is in Elysium the dwelling place of the blessed after death, a state or place of ideal happiness, perfect bliss.

embargo A government order prohibiting the movement of merchant ships into or out of its ports.

embedded Surrounded tightly or firmly; enveloped or enclosed.

emblem A sign, design, or figure that identifies or represents someone or something.

embody **1.** To invest (a spiritual entity) with a body or with bodily form; render incarnate; make corporeal. **2.** To give a tangible, bodily, or concrete form to (an abstract concept) or to be an example of or express (an idea, principle, etc. **embodies, embodied, embodying, self-embodying.**

embody **1.** To invest (a spiritual entity) with a body or with bodily form; render incarnate; make corporeal. **2.** To give a tangible, bodily, or concrete form to (an abstract concept) or to be an example of or express (an idea, principle, etc. **embodies, embodied, embodying, self-embodying.**

embryo **1.** Any organism in a developmental stage preceding birth. **2.** The beginning or rudimentary stage of anything.

employment The purpose for which something is used.

empowered 1. To invest with power, especially legal power or official authority. **2.** To equip or supply with an ability; enable; make powerful.

enamoured Filled or inflamed with love. captivated.

enfranchise To set free; liberate, as from slavery.

enginery Skilful or artful contrivance.

engross 1. To devote (oneself) fully to; consume all of one's attention or time. **2.** To acquire the entire use of, take altogether to itself; to occupy entirely, monopolise. **engrossed, engrossing.**

enigma 1. A puzzling or mystifying saying, in which some known thing is concealed under obscure language; an obscure question; a riddle. **2.** Something seemingly having no explanation; a puzzling or inexplicable occurrence or situation. **enigma's, Enigma, Enigma's, enigmaed.**

enigmatic Resembling an enigma; perplexing; mysterious.

enlighten To give intellectual or spiritual light to; instruct; impart knowledge to. **enlightened, enlightening, enlightenment.**

enshrine To place or enclose in or as if in a shrine. **enshrined, enshrining.**

ensorcelling Enchanting, bewitching.

enthroned Seated on a throne; raised to a lofty position; exalted.

entomb To place in or as if in a tomb; bury; inter. **entombed, entombing**

environs A surrounding area, especially of a city.

ephemeral Lasting for only a short time; transitory; short-lived.

epicure A person who cultivates a refined taste; connoisseur.

epiphany 1. An appearance or manifestation, *esp.* of a deity. **2.** A sudden intuitive perception of or insight into the reality or essential meaning of something. **epiphanies.**

epitome A person or thing that is typical of or possesses to a high degree the features of a whole class; embodiment, quintessence.

equate **1.** To consider, treat, or depict as equal or equivalent. **2.** To state the equality of or between (things). **equates, equating.**

errant **1.** Wandering in search of adventure. **2.** Straying from the proper course or standards. **3.** Moving in an aimless or lightly changing manner.

eternise To make eternal; perpetuate; immortalise. **eternised.**

ether **1.** The regions of space beyond the earth's atmosphere; the heavens. **2.** The element believed in ancient and medieval civilizations to fill all space above the sphere of the moon and to compose the stars and planets. **3.** A hypothetical medium formerly believed to permeate all space, and through which light and other electromagnetic radiation were thought to move. **ether's.**

evanescent **1.** Vanishing; fading away; fleeting. **2.** Tending to become imperceptible; scarcely perceptible.

exalt To raise in rank, character, or status; elevate. **exalted.**

exults Shows or feels a lively or triumphant joy; rejoices exceedingly; is highly elated or jubilant. **exulting, exultant, exultation.**

faery Faerylike; of the nature of a faery (one of a class of supernatural beings, generally conceived as having a diminutive human form and possessing magical powers with which they intervene in human affairs); magical. **faeries', faery-small.**

fancy **1.** Imagination or fantasy, *esp.* as exercised in a capricious manner. **2.** A mental image or conception. **3.** An idea or opinion with little foundation; illusion. **4.** A caprice; whim. **5.** A sudden or irrational liking for a person or thing. **fancy's, Fancy's, fancies.**

fane A temple; sanctuary. **fanes.**

fantasia **1.** A composition in fanciful or irregular form or style. **2.** Something considered to be unreal, weird, exotic, or grotesque.

fathom To penetrate to the truth of; comprehend; understand.

felicity An instance of great happiness; bliss. **felicity's, felicities.**

fell Of an inhumanly cruel nature; fierce; destructive. (All other references to the word are as the past tense of *fall.*)

ferment 1. A state of agitation or of turbulent change or development. **2.** A process of nature involving the addition of yeasts, moulds and certain bacteria (to liquids or solids) causing an effervescence or internal commotion, with evolution of heat, in the substance operated on, and a resulting alteration of its properties.

fiat Official sanction; authoritative permission or order; command.

figured Decorated or patterned with a design.

figure *n.* **1.** The form or shape of anything; appearance, aspect. **2.** The human form, *esp.* as regards size or shape. **3.** A representation or likeness of the human form. **4.** An emblem, type, symbol. **5.** An amount or value expressed in numbers. **6.** A written symbol other than a letter. *v.* **7.** To compute or calculate. **8.** To represent by a pictorial or sculptured figure, a diagram, or the like; picture or depict. **9.** To shape to; symbolize; represent. **figures, figured, figuring, figure-selves.**

firmament The vault or expanse of the heavens; the sky. **firmaments.**

fissured Split open or apart; cleaved; separated, divided.

forborne Abstained or refrained from (some action or procedure); ceased, desisted from.

foreboding ('s) *n.* **1.** A strong inner feeling or notion of a future misfortune, evil, etc.; presentiment. *adj.* **2.** Foretelling or predicting; indicating beforehand; portending.

formative Giving form or shape; forming; shaping; fashioning; moulding.

formulate To devise or develop, as a method, system, etc. or reduce to or express in a formula.

fortuitous Happening or produced by chance; accidental; lucky; fortunate.

fragment *n.* **1.** A small part broken off or detached from any larger whole. **2.** An incomplete and unfinished piece; portion. **3.** An incomplete or isolated portion; a bit. **fragments, fragment-being, fragment-mirrorings.** *v.* **4.** To break or separate (something) into fragments. **fragmented.**

fragmentary Consisting of small, disconnected parts.

frankincense An aromatic gum resin obtained from African and Asian trees of the genus *Boswellia* and used chiefly as incense and in perfumes.

fraught Filled or charged; attended. **deep-fraught, marvel-fraught, pain-fraught.**

frescoed Painted on fresh moist plaster with pigments dissolved in water. **many-frescoed.**

fretted Ornamented with elaborate patterns or angular designs.

frieze The upper part of the wall of a room, below the cornice, *esp.* one that is decorated. **friezes.**

fringe **1.** A decorative border of thread, cord, or the like, usually hanging loosely from a ravelled edge or strip. **2.** Anything resembling or suggesting this. **3.** An outer edge; margin; periphery. **fringes, fringed.**

Furies "Erinyes, in Greek mythology, the goddesses of vengeance, usually represented as three winged maidens, with snakes in their hair. They pursued criminals, drove them mad, and tormented them in Hades. They were spirits of punishment, avenging wrongs done especially to kindred. In Roman literature they were called Furies." *Glossary and Index of Proper Names in Sri Aurobindo's Works*

futile Having no effective result; unsuccessful; pointless; unimportant. **futility.**

gabled Built with a gable (The generally triangular section of wall at the end of a pitched roof, occupying the space between the two slopes of the roof.).

Gandharva Sri Aurobindo: "The Gandharvas are of the vital plane but they are vital Gods, not Asuras." *Letters on Yoga*

"Soma is the Gandharva, the Lord of the hosts of delight, and guards the true seat of the Deva, the level or plane of the Ananda; *gandharva itthâ padam asya rakshati.* He is the Supreme, standing out from all other beings and over them, other than they and wonderful, *adbhuta*, and as the supreme and transcendent, present in the worlds but exceeding them, he protects in those worlds the births of the gods, *pâti devânâm janimâni adbhutah.* The 'births of the gods' is a common phrase in the Veda by which is meant the manifestation of the divine principles in the cosmos and especially the formation of the godhead in its manifold forms in the human being." *The Secret of the Veda*

". . . in the Veda, Lord of the hosts of delight; in later mythology, the Gandharvas are musicians of heaven, 'beautiful, brave and melodious beings, the artists, musicians, poets and shining warriors of heaven'. . . ." *Glossary and Index of Proper Names in Sri Aurobindo's Works*

Gandharvas.

gargoyle A grotesquely carved face or figure of a human or animal.

genealogy A record or account of the ancestry and descent of a person, family, group, etc.

genii **1.** A rendering of *Arab., jinn*, the collective name of a class of spirits (some good, some evil) supposed to interfere powerfully in human affairs. **2.** Spirits, often appearing in human form, that when summoned carry out the wishes of the summoner.

ghauts A wide set of steps descending to a river.

gilded **1.** Made from or covered with gold. **2.** Having a deep golden colour.

glade An open space in a forest. **glades.**

gleam *n.* **1.** A brief beam or flash of light. **2.** A brief or dim indication; a trace. **3.** The appearance of radiant beauty. **Gleam, gleams.** *v.* **4.** To emit a gleam; flash or glow briefly or faintly. **gleams, gleamed, gleaming, gleam-ridge.**

glimmer *n.* **1.** A dim or intermittent flicker or flash of light. **2.** A slight suggestion or vague understanding. *v.* **3.** To shine faintly; twinkle, shimmer, or flicker. **glimmers, glimmered, glimmering, glimmerings, glimmer-realms, many-glimmered.**

glint **1.** A tiny, quick flash of light. **2.** A brief or slight manifestation; inkling; trace.

glut *n.* **1.** An excessive amount, an oversupply. *v.* **2.** To feed or fill to satiety. **glutted.**

gnarled Having gnarls; knotty or misshapen.

goad *n.* **1.** A long stick with a pointed end used for prodding animals. **2.** An agent or means of prodding or urging; a stimulus. *v.* **3.** To prod or urge with or as if with a long pointed stick. **goads.**

goblin A grotesque sprite or elf that is mischievous or malicious toward people. **goblins, goblin-wizened.**

Godhead Sri Aurobindo: ". . . the Godhead is all that is universe and all that is in the universe and all that is more than the universe. The Gita lays stress first on his supracosmic existence. For otherwise the mind would miss its highest goal and remain turned towards the cosmic only or else attached to some partial experience of the Divine in the cosmos. It lays stress next on his universal existence in which all moves and acts. For that is the justification of the cosmic effort and that is the vast spiritual self-awareness in which the Godhead self-seen as the Time-Spirit does his universal works. Next it insists with a certain austere emphasis on the acceptance of the Godhead as the divine inhabitant in the human body. For he is the Immanent in all existences, and if the indwelling divinity is not recognised, not only will the divine meaning of individual existence be missed, the urge to our supreme spiritual possibilities deprived of its greatest force, but the relations of soul with soul in humanity will be left petty, limited and egoistic. Finally, it insists at great length on the divine manifestation in all things in the universe and affirms the derivation of all that is from the nature, power and light of the one Godhead." *Essays on the Gita*

"The Godhead is one in his transcendence, one all-supporting Self of things, one in the unity of his cosmic nature. These three are one Godhead; all derives from him, all becomes from his being, all is eternal portion or temporal expression of the Eternal." *Essays on the Gita*

"This Godhead is one in all things that are, the self who lives in all and the self in whom all live and move; therefore man has to discover his spiritual unity with all creatures, to see all in the self and the self in all beings, even to see all things and creatures as himself, *âtmaupamyena sarvatra*, and accordingly think, feel and act in all his mind, will and living. This Godhead is the origin of all that is here or elsewhere and by his Nature he has become all these innumerable existences, *abhût sarvâni bhûtâni*; therefore man has to see and adore the One in all things animate and inanimate, to worship the manifestation in sun and star and flower, in man and every living creature, in the forms and forces, qualities and powers of Nature, *vâsudevah sarvam iti*." *Essays on the Gita*

godhead, godheads, godhead's.

the godheads of the living Suns,

gorged Glutted to the full, as with food, conquest, etc.

gramarye Occult learning; magic.

grandeur 1. Nobility or greatness of character. **2.** The quality of being magnificent or splendid or grand. **Grandeur, grandeur's, grandeurs.**

grapple *n.* **1.** A struggle or contest in which the participants attempt to clutch or grip each other. *v.* **2.** To try to deal with a problem, etc. **grappled.**

graved Carved, sculpted or engraved.

grisly 1. Causing a shudder or feeling of horror; horrible; gruesome, ghastly. **2.** Formidable, grim.

grotesques Characterized by ludicrous or incongruous distortion, as of appearance or manner; bizarre; outlandish.

Gundhurvas

gurgling Flowing in a broken, irregular, noisy current; emitting a sound as of bubbling liquid.

gust 1. A strong, abrupt rush of wind. **2.** A sudden burst or outburst. **gusts, gusty.**

habitation A place of abode; a residence ; dwelling-place.

haled 1. Pulled, drawn, dragged, or hoisted. **2.** Compelled (someone) to go.

hallowed Regarded as holy; venerated; sacred.

harping Making a musical sound like that of a harp.

haunt *n.* **1.** A place frequently visited. haunts. *v.* **2.** To recur persistently to the consciousness of; remain with. **3.** To visit often; frequent. **4.** To inhabit, visit, or appear to in the form of a ghost or other supernatural being. **haunts, haunted.**

hazard *n.* **1.** An unavoidable danger or risk, even though often foreseeable. **2.** Something causing unavoidable danger, peril, risk, or difficulty. **3.** The absence or lack of predictability; chance; uncertainty. **hazard's, hazards.** *v.* **4.** To expose to hazard or risk. **5.** To venture (something); dare. **6.** To venture upon (anything of doubtful issue). **hazards, hazarded.**

hazardous 1. Full of risk; perilous; risky. **2.** Dependent on chance; uncertain.

hegemony The predominant influence, as of a state, region, or group, over another or others.

hew 1. To cut something by repeated blows, as of an axe. **2.** To make or shape as with an axe. **3.** To sever from a larger or another portion as with a blow. **4.** To cut down with an axe; fell; slay. **hews, hewed, hewn, hewing, hewer, half-hewn, rock-hewn.**

rough-hewn. Shaped out roughly, given crude form to; worked or executed in the rough. (Here in reference to Satyavan's abode.)

hierarchy A system of persons or things arranged in a graded order. **hierarchies, Hierarchies.**

hieratic **1.** Of or associated with sacred persons or their offices or duties. **2.** Constituting or relating to a simplified cursive style of Egyptian hieroglyphics, used in both sacred and secular writings.

hold *n.* **1.** The lower interior part of a ship or airplane where cargo is stored. **2.** The act or a means of grasping. *v.* **3.** To have or keep in the hand; keep fast; grasp. **4.** To bear, sustain, or support, as with the hands or arms, or by any other means. **5.** To contain or be capable of containing. **6.** To keep from departing or getting away. **7.** To withstand stress, pressure, or opposition; to maintain occupation of by force or coercion. **8.** To have in its power, possess, affect, occupy. **9.** To engage in; preside over; carry on. **10.** To have or keep in the mind; think or believe. **11.** To regard or consider. **12.** To keep or maintain a grasp on something. **13.** To maintain one's position against opposition; continue in resistance. **14.** To agree or side (usually followed by with). **holds, holding.**

hold back. **15. a**. To retain possession of; keep back. **b**. To refrain from revealing; withhold. **c**. To refrain from participating or engaging in some activity.

hold up. **16.** To present to notice; expose.

hollow *adj.* **1.** Void or empty space. **2.** Having a cavity, gap, or space within. **3.** *Fig.* Without substance or character; devoid of truth or validity; specious. *n.* **3.** A void space. **4.** A cavity, opening, space, or burrow. **hollows.**

homestead Any dwelling with its land and buildings where a family makes its home. **homestead's.**

huddled Crowded or massed together.

hymn A song of praise or thanksgiving to God or a deity.

hypothesis **1.** A suggested explanation for a group of facts or phenomena, either accepted as a basis for further verification (working hypothesis) or accepted as likely to be true. **2.** An assumption used in an argument without its being endorsed; a supposition.

icon **1.** An image; a representation. **2.** A sign or representation that stands for its object by virtue of a resemblance or analogy to it. **icons.**

ideal *n.* **1.** A conception of something in its absolute perfection. *adj.* **2.** One that is regarded as a standard or model of perfection or excellence. **Ideal, ideal's, Ideal's, ideals.**

Sri Aurobindo: ". . . ideals and idealists are necessary; ideals are the savour and sap of life, idealists the most powerful diviners and assistants of its purposes." *The Human Cycle*

"Ideals are truths that have not yet effected themselves for man, the realities of a higher plane of existence which have yet to fulfil themselves on this lower plane of life and matter, our present field of operation." *Essays in Philosophy and Yoga*

"Certainly, ideals are not the ultimate Reality, for that is too high and vast for any ideal to envisage; they are aspects of it thrown out in the world-consciousness as a basis for the workings of the world-power. But they are primary, the actual workings secondary. They are nearer to the Reality and therefore always more real, forcible and complete than the facts which are their partial reflection." *Essays in Philosophy and Yoga*

"The Ideal is an eternal Reality which we have not yet realised in the conditions of our own being, not a non-existent which the Eternal and Divine has not yet grasped and only we imperfect beings have glimpsed and mean to create." *The Life Divine*

"Ideals are truths that have not yet effected themselves for man, the realities of a higher plane of existence which have yet to fulfil themselves on this lower plane of life and matter, our present field of operation. To the pragmatical intellect which takes its stand upon the ever-changing present, ideals are not truths, not realities, they are at most potentialities of future truth and only become real when they are visible in the external fact as work of force accomplished. But to the mind which is able to draw back from the flux of force in the material universe, to the consciousness which is not imprisoned in its own workings or carried along in their flood but is able to envelop, hold and comprehend them, to the soul that is not merely the subject and instrument of the world-force but can reflect something of that Master-Consciousness which controls and uses it, the ideal present to its inner vision is a greater reality than the changing fact obvious to its outer senses. *The Supramental Manifestation*

Certainly, ideals are not the ultimate Reality, for that is too high and vast for any ideal to envisage; they are aspects of it thrown out in the world-consciousness as a basis for the workings of the world-power. But they are primary, the actual workings secondary. They are nearer to the Reality and therefore always more real, forcible and complete than the facts which are their partial reflection. Reflections themselves of the Real, they again are reflected in the more concrete workings of our existence. *The Supramental Manifestation*

idol   1. An image or other material object representing a deity to which religious worship is addressed. **2.** A mere image or semblance of something visible but without substance, as a phantom. **3.** A false conception or notion; fallacy. **Idol, idols.**

illume   1. To illuminate; make lighter or brighter, *esp. poetic.* **2.** To enlighten the mind. **illumes.**

illuminate   One who has or professes to have an unusual degree of enlightenment.

illusion   1. The condition of being deceived by a false perception, belief or appearance. **2.** Something, such as a fantastic plan or desire that causes an erroneous belief or perception; as a deceptive apparition etc. **Illusion, illusion's, Illusion's, illusions, illusion-makers.**

Sri Aurobindo: "In fact it [the world] is not an illusion in the sense of an imposition of something baseless and unreal on the consciousness, but a misinterpretation by the conscious mind and sense and a falsifying misuse of manifested existence." *Letters on Yoga*

illusive Producing, produced by, or based on illusion; deceptive or unreal.

imager Something or someone that produces images or representations of.

immanent Existing or remaining within; inherent.

The Immanent. *Theol.* (of the Deity) Indwelling or abiding in the universe, time, etc.

Sri Aurobindo: "He is the Cosmic Spirit and all-creating Energy around us; he is the Immanent within us. All that is is he, and he is the More than all that is, and we ourselves, though we know it not, are being of his being, force of his force, conscious with a consciousness derived from his; even our mortal existence is made out of his substance and there is an immortal within us that is a spark of the Light and Bliss that are for ever. No matter whether by knowledge, works, love or any other means, to become aware of this truth of our being, to realise it, to make it effective here or elsewhere is the object of all Yoga." *The Synthesis of Yoga*

"It [the psychic] is constantly in contact with the immanent Divine -- the Divine secret in the individual." *Letters on Yoga*

"Next it [the Gita] insists with a certain austere emphasis on the acceptance of the Godhead as the divine inhabitant in the human body. For he is the Immanent in all existences, and if the indwelling divinity is not recognised, not only will the divine meaning of individual existence be missed, the urge to our supreme spiritual possibilities deprived of its greatest force, but the relations of soul with soul in humanity will be left petty, limited and egoistic." *Essays on the Gita*

"There results an integral vision of the Divine Existent at once as the transcendent Reality, supracosmic origin of cosmos, as the impersonal Self of all things, calm continent of the cosmos, and as the immanent Divinity in all beings, personalities, objects, powers and qualities, the Immanent who is the constituent self, the effective nature and the inward and outward becoming of all existences." *Essays on the Gita*

immensitudes Sri Aurobindo: "I take upon myself the right to coin new words. 'Immensitudes' is not any more fantastic than 'infinitudes' to pair 'infinity'." **immensitude, Immensitudes.**

immune Totally protected against, or naturally resistant to, a disease; injury *etc.* **Immune, immunity.**

immutable Not subject or susceptible to change. **Immutable, immutable's, immutably, immutability.**

impalpable 1. Not perceptible to the touch; intangible. **2.** Difficult to perceive or grasp by the mind.

impassive 1. Without emotion; apathetic; unmoved. **2.** Calm; serene. **3.** Not subject to suffering; unaffected. **impassively.**

impeccable Faultless, unerring, flawless, irreproachable.

imperious Regal; imperial; sovereign; majestic.

implacable Not to be appeased, mollified, or pacified; inexorable. **implacably.**

impotent Lacking sufficient strength or ability; powerless to achieve.

imps Small demons or devils; mischievous sprites.

impunity Immunity from detrimental effects, as of an action.

inapt 1. Without aptitude or capacity; incapable. **2.** Not inclined or disposed.

incalculable 1. Too great to be calculated or reckoned. **2.** Impossible to foresee; unpredictable. **Incalculable, incalculable's.** (Sri Aurobindo also employs the word as a *n.*)

incarnate *adj.* **1.** Embodied in flesh; given a bodily, *esp.* a human, form. **2.** Personified or typified, as a quality or idea. *v.* **3.** Invested with bodily nature and form. **4.** To realize in action or fact; actualize. **incarnated, incarnating.**

Incarnate The One embodied in flesh. **Incarnate's.**

incertitude Absence of confidence; doubt; uncertainty. **incertitudes.**

Sri Aurobindo: [referring to the line] "The incertitude of man's proud confident thought."

"'Uncertainty' would mean that the thought was confident but uncertain of itself, which would be a contradiction. 'Incertitude' means that its truth is uncertain in spite of its proud confidence in itself." *Letters on Savitri* — 1936

incognito A concealed identity.

incoherent Without logical or meaningful connection; disjointed; rambling. **incoherence, incoherencies.**

incommunicable Impossible to be transmitted or communicated. **Incommunicable.**

Inconscience Sri Aurobindo: "The Inconscience is an inverse reproduction of the supreme superconscience: it has the same absoluteness of being and automatic action, but in a vast involved trance; it is being lost in itself, plunged in its own abyss of infinity." *The Life Divine*

"All aspects of the omnipresent Reality have their fundamental truth in the Supreme Existence. Thus even the aspect or power of Inconscience, which seems to be an opposite, a negation of the eternal Reality, yet corresponds to a Truth held in itself by the self-aware and all-conscious Infinite. It is, when we look closely at it, the Infinite's power of plunging the consciousness into a trance of self-involution, a self-oblivion of the Spirit veiled in its own abysses where nothing is manifest but all inconceivably is and can emerge from that ineffable latency. In the heights of Spirit this state of cosmic or infinite trance-sleep appears to our cognition as a luminous uttermost Superconscience: at the other end of being it offers itself to cognition as the Spirit's potency of presenting to itself the opposites of its own truths of being, -- an abyss of non-existence, a profound Night of inconscience, a fathomless swoon of insensibility from which yet all forms of being, consciousness and delight of existence can manifest themselves, -- but they appear in limited terms, in slowly emerging and increasing self-formulations, even in contrary terms of themselves; it is the play of a secret all-being, all-delight, all-knowledge, but it observes the rules of its own self-oblivion, self-opposition, self-limitation until it is ready to surpass it. This is the Inconscience and Ignorance that we see at work in the material universe. It is not a denial, it is one term, one formula of the infinite and eternal Existence." *The Life Divine*

"Once consciousnesses separated from the one consciousness, they fell inevitably into Ignorance and the last result of Ignorance was Inconscience." *Letters on Yoga*

inconscience.

Inconscient Sri Aurobindo: "The Inconscient and the Ignorance may be mere empty abstractions and can be dismissed as irrelevant jargon if one has not come in collision with them or plunged into their dark and bottomless reality. But to me they are realities, concrete powers whose resistance is present everywhere and at all times in its tremendous and boundless mass." *Letters on Savitri*

". . . in its actual cosmic manifestation the Supreme, being the Infinite and not bound by any limitation, can manifest in Itself, in its consciousness of innumerable possibilities, something that seems to be the opposite of itself, something in which there can be Darkness, Inconscience, Inertia, Insensibility, Disharmony and Disintegration. It is this that we see at the basis of the material world and speak of nowadays as the Inconscient -- the Inconscient Ocean of the Rigveda in which the One was hidden and arose in the form of this universe -- or, as it is sometimes called, the non-being, Asat." *Letters on Yoga*

"The Inconscient itself is only an involved state of consciousness which like the Tao or Shunya, though in a different way, contains all things suppressed within it so that under a pressure from above or within all can evolve out of it -- 'an inert Soul with a somnambulist Force'." *Letters on Yoga*

"The Inconscient is the last resort of the Ignorance." *Letters on Yoga*

"The body, we have said, is a creation of the Inconscient and itself inconscient or at least subconscient in parts of itself and much of its hidden action; but what we call the Inconscient is an appearance, a dwelling place, an instrument of a secret Consciousness or a Superconscient which has created the miracle we call the universe." *Essays in Philosophy and Yoga*

"The Inconscient is a sleep or a prison, the conscient a round of strivings without ultimate issue or the wanderings of a dream: we must wake into the superconscious where all darkness of night and half-lights cease in the self-luminous bliss of the Eternal." *The Life Divine*

"Men have not learnt yet to recognise the Inconscient on which the whole material world they see is built, or the Ignorance of which their whole nature including their knowledge is built; they think that these words are only abstract metaphysical jargon flung about by the philosophers in their clouds or laboured out in long and wearisome books like *The Life Divine. Letters on Savitri*

"Is it really a fact that even the ordinary reader would not be able to see any difference between the Inconscient and Ignorance unless the difference is expressly explained to him? This is not a matter of philosophical terminology but of common sense and the understood meaning of English words. One would say 'even the inconscient stone' but one would not say, as one might of a child, 'the ignorant stone'. One must first be conscious before one can be ignorant. What is true is that the ordinary reader might not be familiar with the philosophical content of the word Inconscient and might not be familiar with the Vedantic idea of the Ignorance as the power behind the manifested world. But I don't see how I can acquaint him with these things in a single line, even with the most. illuminating image or symbol. He might wonder, if he were Johnsonianly minded, how an Inconscient could be teased or how it could wake Ignorance. I am afraid, in the absence of a miracle of inspired poetical exegesis flashing through my mind, he will have to be left wondering." *Letters on Savitri*

inconscient, Inconscient's.

inconstant Changing or varying, especially often and without discernible pattern or reason.

indecipherable **1.** Not decipherable; illegible. **2.** Not understandable; incomprehensible. **Indecipherable.**

indeterminate   Not precisely fixed, as to extent, size, nature, or number. **Indeterminate.**

indifferent **1.** Having no marked feeling for or against. **2.** Without interest or feeling in regard to something; unbiased, impartial, neutral; fair; unconcerned, unmoved, apathetic. **3.** Being neither good nor bad; neutral.

indigent   Deficient in what is requisite; poor; impoverished.

indolence   Habitual laziness; sloth.

indomitable   Incapable of being overcome, subdued, or vanquished; unconquerable. **indomitably.**

ineffable   Incapable of being expressed; indescribable or unutterable. **Ineffable, Ineffable's.**

The Ineffable: Sri Aurobindo: "It is this essential indeterminability of the Absolute that translates itself into our consciousness through the fundamental negating positives of our spiritual experience, the immobile immutable Self, the Nirguna Brahman, the Eternal without qualities, the pure featureless One Existence, the Impersonal, the Silence void of activities, the Non-being, the Ineffable and the Unknowable. On the other side it is the essence and source of all determinations, and this dynamic essentiality manifests to us through the fundamental affirming positives in which the Absolute equally meets us; for it is the Self that becomes all things, the Saguna Brahman, the Eternal with infinite qualities, the One who is the Many, the infinite Person who is the source and foundation of all persons and personalities, the Lord of creation, the Word, the Master of all works and action; it is that which being known all is known: these affirmatives correspond to those negatives. For it is not possible in a supramental cognition to split asunder the two sides of the One Existence, -- even to speak of them as sides is excessive, for they are in each other, their co-existence or one-existence is eternal and their powers sustaining each other found the self-manifestation of the Infinite." *The Life Divine*

"Ishwara is Brahman the Reality, Self, Spirit, revealed as possessor, enjoyer of his own self-existence, creator of the universe and one with it, Pantheos, and yet superior to it, the Eternal, the Infinite, the Ineffable, the Divine Transcendence." *The Life Divine*

"The Absolute is for us the Ineffable." *The Life Divine*

"A transcendent Bliss, unimaginable and inexpressible by the mind and speech, is the nature of the Ineffable. That broods immanent and secret in the whole universe and in everything in the universe. Its presence is described as a secret ether of the bliss of being, of which the Scripture says that, if this were not, none could for a moment breathe or live. And this spiritual bliss is here also in our hearts." *The Synthesis of Yoga*

inert   **1.** Unable to move or act; immobile, unmoving, lifeless, motionless. **2.** Inactive or sluggish by habit or nature. **inertness.**

inertia Inertness, *esp.* with regard to effort, motion, action, and the like; inactivity; sluggishness. **Inertia, Inertia's.**

inexorable Not capable of being persuaded by entreaty; relentless. **inexorably.**

inexplicable   Difficult or impossible to explain or account for. **inexplicably.**

inextricable   Intricately involved; incapable of being disentangled, loosed, or undone. **inextricably.**

infallible 1. Incapable of failure or error. **2.** Not liable to failure; certain; sure. **3.** Absolutely trustworthy or sure. **4.** Unfailing in effectiveness or operation; certain. **infallibly, infallibility.**

infamies Infamous, shameful, or utterly disgraceful acts.

infernal Fiendish; diabolical.

Inferno A place or condition suggestive of hell, especially with respect to human suffering or death; the infernal regions. **Inferno's.**

the Infinite   A designation of the Deity or the absolute Being; God. **Infinite's.**

Sri Aurobindo: "The Infinite is not a sum of things, it is That which is all things and more." *The Life Divine*

"Even the words Eternal and Infinite are only symbolic expressions through which the mind feels without grasping some vague impression of this Supreme." *Essays Divine and Human*

"Yet the highest power and manifestation is only a very partial revelation of the Infinite; even the whole universe is informed by only one degree of his greatness, illumined by one ray of his splendour, glorious with a faint hint of his delight and beauty." *Essays on the Gita*

The Mother (to a young person): "It is very simple, as you will see. 1) The Infinite is the inexhaustible storehouse of forces. The individual is a battery, a storage cell which runs down after use. Consecration is the wire that connects the individual battery to the infinite reserve of forces. Or 2) The Infinite is the river that flows without cease; the individual is the little pond that dries up slowly in the sun. Consecration is the canal that connects the river to the pond and prevents the pond from drying up." *The Mother - Collected Works, Centenary Ed., Vol. 16 - Some Answers from the Mother*

Infinite, the triune *See* **triune Infinite.**

Infinitesimal Immeasurably or incalculably minute. **Infinitesimal's.**

infinitude   **1.** The state or quality of being infinite; boundless. **2.** An immeasurably large quantity, number, or extent. **infinitudes, Infinitude, Infinitudes.**

ingenious   1. Characterised by cleverness or originality of invention or construction. **2.** Cleverly inventive or resourceful. **ingeniously.**

ingenuity   1. Inventive skill or imagination; cleverness. **2.** An ingenious or imaginative contrivance.

inhabit   1. To live or dwell in (a place), as people or animals. **2.** To exist or be situated within; dwell in. **inhabited, inhabiting, inhabitant, Inhabitant, inhabitants, all-inhabiting.**

inhuman Lacking humane feelings, such as sympathy, understanding, etc.; cruel; brutal. Also *fig.*

iniquity Gross injustice or wickedness; infamy, depravity. **iniquities.**

initiate *Ppla.***1.** Instructed in or introduced to secret or sacred knowledge. *n.***2.** A novice, beginner. **Initiate.**

initiative An introductory act or step; leading action.

inly 1. In an inward manner; inwardly. **2.** Intimately; deeply within.

inscrutable 1. Difficult or nearly impossible to fathom or understand; impenetrable. **2.** Incapable of being seen through physically; physically impenetrable.

interlude An intervening episode, feature, or period of time.

intimation A subtle and inner hint or suggestion; indication. **intimations.**

intones Speaks or recites in a singing voice, *esp.* in monotone; chants. **intoning.**

intuitive 1. Obtained through intuition rather than from reasoning or observation. **2.** *Fig.* Concerning spiritual vision or perception.

invincible Incapable of being overcome or defeated; unconquerable. **invincibly.**

inviolate Unable to be violated or profaned; undisturbed; intact.

invulnerable 1. Immune to attack; impregnable. **2.** Impossible to damage, injure, or wound.

irrational 1. Not endowed with reason. **2.** Inconsistent with reason or logic; illogical; absurd.

jar A wide-mouthed container that is usually cylindrical, made of glass or earthenware, and without handles. Also *fig.* **jars.**

jar 1. A harsh, grating sound. **2.** A sudden unpleasant effect upon the mind or feelings; shock. **3.** A quarrel or disagreement, especially a minor one. **jars, jarring.**

jets A stream of a liquid, gas, or small solid particles forcefully shooting forth from a nozzle, orifice, etc. Also *fig.*

jinns

keel 1. The principal structural member of a ship or boat, running lengthwise along the center line from bow to stern, to which the frames are attached. **2.** A poetic word for ship.

key-book A book or other text containing the system or explanatory scheme for the interpretation of a cipher, code, or other composition of hidden or veiled meaning.

kindle 1. To start (a fire); cause (a flame, blaze, etc.) to begin burning; often *fig.* **2.** To light up, illuminate, or make bright. **3.** To arouse or be aroused; call forth (emotions, feelings, and responses); **4.** To begin to burn as combustible matter, a light, fire, or flame. **kindles, kindled, kindling.**

kinetic Of, relating to, or produced by motion.

labyrinthine Resembling a labyrinth in complexity.

laden 1. Filled or covered abundantly. **2.** Burdened; loaded down.

laggard Moving, developing, or responding slowly; sluggish; dilatory; backward.lambent **1.** Flickering lightly over or on a surface. **2.** Having a gentle glow; luminous.

lapis lazuli A deep blue mineral composed mainly of lazarite with smaller quantities of other minerals, used mainly as a gem or as a pigment.

lapped Lifted with or as with the tongue, licked.

lapped 1. Enveloped in something. **2.** Wrapped or wound around (something); encircled.

lapse 1. An accidental or temporary decline or deviation from an expected or accepted condition or state; a temporary falling or slipping from a previous standard. **2.** A gradual decline or a drop to a lower degree, condition, or state. **3.** A gradual deterioration or decline; regression. **4.** The act of falling, slipping, sliding, etc. slowly or by degrees. **lapsed, lapsing, far-lapsing.**

lattice An open framework made of strips of metal, wood, or similar material overlapped or overlaid in a regular, usually crisscross pattern. **lattices, lattice-window.**

leviathan A monstrous sea creature symbolizing evil.

licence Excessive freedom; lack of due restraint.

limned Depicted by or as painting or drawing. **half-limned.**

lists **1.** Arenas for jousting tournaments or other contests. **2.** A place of combat.

logarithmic Of or pertaining to a logarithm or logarithms, i.e. the exponent or power to which a base number must be raised to equal a given number.

logic **1.** The science that investigates the principles governing correct or reliable inference. **2.** The system or principles of reasoning applicable to any branch of knowledge or study. **3.** Convincing forcefulness; inexorable truth or persuasiveness. **logic's.**

lolled **1.** Leaned, or lounged in a lazy or relaxed manner. **2.** (of the tongue) Hung down or out. **lolling.**

lotus Any aquatic plant of the genus *Nelumbo*, of the water lily family, having shieldlike leaves and showy, solitary flowers usually projecting above the water. **lotuses, lotus-bud, lotus-cup, lotus-heart, lotus-leaf, lotus-pools, lotus-throne.**

blue lotus of the Idea.

Sri Aurobindo: "It can be taken as the (Avatar) incarnation on the mental plane." *Visions of Champaklal*

lotus (as chakra) Sri Aurobindo: "This arrangement of the psychic body is reproduced in the physical with the spinal column as a rod and the ganglionic centres as the chakras which rise up from the bottom of the column, where the lowest is attached, to the brain and find their summit in the *brahmarandhra* at the top of the skull. These chakras or lotuses, however, are in physical man closed or only partly open, with

the consequence that only such powers and only so much of them are active in him as are sufficient for his ordinary physical life, and so much mind and soul only is at play as will accord with its need. This is the real reason, looked at from the mechanical point of view, why the embodied soul seems so dependent on the bodily and nervous life, -- though the dependence is neither so complete nor so real as it seems. The whole energy of the soul is not at play in the physical body and life, the secret powers of mind are not awake in it, the bodily and nervous energies predominate. But all the while the supreme energy is there, asleep; it is said to be coiled up and slumbering like a snake, -- therefore it is called the *kundalinî sakti*, -- in the lowest of the chakras, in the mûlâdhâra."
The Synthesis of Yoga

"One can speak of the chakras only in reference to yoga. In ordinary people the chakras are not open, it is only when they do sadhana that the chakras open. For the chakras are the centres of the inner consciousness and belong originally to the subtle body. So much as is active in ordinary people is very little -- for in them it is the outer consciousness that is active." *Letters on Yoga*

"Within us, there are two centres of the Purusha, the inner Soul through which he touches us to our awakening; there is the Purusha in the lotus of the heart which opens upward all our powers and the Purusha in the thousand-petalled lotus whence descend through the thought and will, opening the third eye in us, the lightnings of vision and the fire of the divine energy. The bliss existence may come to us through either one of these centres. When the lotus of the heart breaks open, we feel a divine joy, love and peace expanding in us like a flower of light which irradiates the whole being." *The Synthesis of Yoga*

"The lotus of the eternal knowledge and the eternal perfection is a bud closed and folded up within us. It opens swiftly or gradually, petal by petal, through successive realisations, once the mind of man begins to turn towards the Eternal, once his heart, no longer compressed and confined by attachment to finite appearances, becomes enamoured, in whatever degree, of the Infinite." *The Synthesis of Yoga*

"The colours of the lotuses and the numbers of petals are respectively, from bottom to top: -- (1) the Muladhara or physical consciousness centre, four petals, red; (2) the abdominal centre, six petals, deep purple red; (3) the navel centre, ten petals, violet; (4) the heart centre, twelve petals, golden pink; (5) the throat centre, sixteen petals, grey; (6) the forehead centre between the eye-brows, two petals, white; (7) the thousand-petalled lotus above the head, blue with gold light around. The functions are, according to our yoga, -- (1) commanding the physical consciousness and the subconscient; (2) commanding the small vital movements, the little greeds, lusts, desires, the small sense-movements; (3) commanding the larger life-forces and the passions and larger desire-movements; (4) commanding the higher emotional being with the psychic deep behind it; (5) commanding expression and all externalisation of the mind movements and mental forces; (6) commanding thought, will, vision; (7) commanding the higher thinking mind and the illumined mind and opening upwards to the intuition and overmind. The seventh is sometimes or by some identified with the brain, but that is an error -- the brain is only a channel of communication situated between the thousand-petalled and the forehead centre. The former is sometimes called the void centre, *sunya* , either because it is not in the body, but in the apparent void above or because rising above the head one enters first into the silence of the self or spiritual being."
Letters on Yoga

lucent **1.** Giving off light; luminous. **2.** Translucent; clear. **lucency.**

lucid **1.** Transmitting light; able to be seen through with clarity. **2.** Shining or glowing. **lucidities.**

lure *n.* **1.** Something that tempts or attract   An expanse of land or water. **tracts, tract-memories, flower-tracts.** with the promise of pleasure or reward. **lures.** *v.* **2.** To attract, tempt, entice. **lures, lured, luring.**

lurk **1.** To lie in wait, as in ambush. **2.** To exist unperceived or unsuspected. **lurks, lurked, lurking.**

lustrous Having a sheen or glow; gleaming with or as if with brilliant light; radiant; shining; luminous. **star-lustrous.**

lyre A musical instrument of ancient Greece consisting of a sound box made typically from a turtle shell, with two curved arms connected by a yoke from which strings are stretched to the body, used especially to accompany singing and recitation. **lyres.**

Madra "Name of an ancient country and its people in northwestern India, mentioned in the *Mahabaharata.* The territory extended from the River Beas to the Chenab or perhaps as far as the Jhelum. Savitri's father Asvapati was king of this country. (Dow.)" *Glossary and Index of Proper Names in Sri Aurobindo's Works*

Madra's.

mage A magician or sorcerer.

Mage Sri Aurobindo: " . . . the supreme Mage, the divine Magician, . . ." [the Lord] *The Life Divine.*

magnanimity Liberality in bestowing gifts; extremely liberal and generous of spirit; generosity or nobility of mind, character, etc.

malignant 1. Showing great malevolence; disposed to do evil. **2.** Very dangerous or harmful in influence or effect.

mandate An authoritative command or instruction.

manifest A document.

manifest *v.* **1.** To show or demonstrate plainly; reveal, display. **manifested.** *adj.* **2.** Readily noticed or perceived; evident; obvious; apparent; plain; visible. **manifesting.**

march *n.* **1.** The steady forward movement of a body of troops. **2.** Steady forward movement or progression. Also *fig.* **marches, marchings, sun-march.** *v.* **3.** To walk steadily and rhythmically forward in step with others, as soldiers on parade; advance in step in an organized body. **4.** To proceed directly and purposefully; to go forward; advance; proceed. **5.** To progress steadily onward; advance. Also *fig.* **marches, marched, marching.**

marge *Poet.* margin, edge, material or immaterial.

mastering Controlling.

mean **1.** Low or poor in quality or grade; inferior. **2.** Ignoble; base. **3.** Of little importance or consequence. **meanest.**

mean To have as its sense or signification; signify. **means, meant.**

measure *n.* **1.** A unit of standard of measurement. **2.** The extent, quantity, dimensions, etc. of (something), ascertained *esp.* by comparison with a standard. **3.** Bounds or limits. **4.** A definite or known quality or quantity measured out. **5.** A short rhythmical movement or arrangement, as in poetry or music. **measures.** *v.* **6.** To determine the size, amount, etc. **7.** To estimate the relative amount, value, etc., of, by comparison with some standard. **8.** To travel or move over as if measuring. **measured, measuring.**

merge To become combined, united, swallowed up or absorbed; lose identity by uniting or blending. **merges, merged, merging.**

metres The rhythmic arrangement of syllables in verse, usually according to the number and kind of feet in a line.

mime To imitate (a person or manner), especially for satirical effect. **mimes.**

mimicry The act, practice, or art of mimicking.

minaret (s) A tall slender tower attached to a mosque, having one or more projecting balconies from which a muezzin summons the people to prayer.

minister A high officer of state appointed to head an executive or administrative department of government. **ministers.**

minstrelsies Minstrels' songs, ballads, etc.

minutiae Small or trivial details.

miracle-monger A compound word denoting a person promoting something undesirable or discreditable, in this instance, miracles.

mire **1.** Deep slimy soil or mud. **2.** An area of wet, soggy, muddy ground; a bog.

mirth Gaiety or jollity, *esp.* when accompanied by laughter.

mission *n.* **1.** The business with which a person or a body of persons is charged. **2.** An assigned or self-imposed duty or task. *v.* **3.** To send forth to someone. **missioned.**

mitred Wearing a liturgical headdress like one worn by a bishop or abbot, in most western churches consisting of a tall pointed cleft cap with two bands hanging down at the back as a symbol of great holiness or dignity.

mnemonics *n.* Devices, such as formulas or rhymes, used as aids in remembering. *adj.* **mnemonic.** Relating to, assisting, or intended to assist the memory.

mock *v.* **1.** To attack or treat with ridicule, contempt, or derision; to jeer, scoff. **2.** To ridicule or jeer by imitation of speech or action. **3.** To frustrate the hopes of; disappoint; delude. **mocks, mocked, mocking, mockst.** *adj.* **4.** Feigned; not real; sham; counterfeit; imitation.

mosaic **1.** A picture or decorative design made by setting small colored pieces, as of stone or tile, into a surface. **2.** Something resembling such a picture or decoration in composition, *esp.* in being made up of diverse elements.

motive *n.* **1.** An emotion, desire, physiological need, or similar impulse that acts as an incitement to action. **motives.** *adj.* **2.** Of or constituting an incitement to action. **3.** In art, literature and music: A motif (a recurring subject, theme, idea). **motived, motiveless.** *v.* **4.** To incite; motivate. **motives.**

mould *n.* **1.** An often hollow matrix or form by which something is shaped; a model, a pattern. **2.** Bodily form, body. Chiefly *poet.* **3.** *Poetic,* the earth. **moulds, moulders.** *v.* **4.** To work into a shape; fashion a material into a form. Chiefly *poet.* **5.** To shape of form in or on a mould. **moulds, moulded, moulding.** *adj.* **moulding. 6.** Forming, shaping. **moulded. 7.** Shaped or cast in a mould; made according to a mould; cut or shaped to a mould.

mured Immured; imprisoned; shut in, secluded or confined.

Muse *Myth.* Any of the nine daughters of Mnemosyne and Zeus, each of whom presided over a different art or science.

Sri Aurobindo: ". The mystic Muse is more of an inspired Bacchante of the Dionysian wine than an orderly housewife." *Letters on Savitri*

muse *n.* **1.** A state of abstraction or contemplation; reverie. **2.** The goddess or the power regarded as inspiring a poet, artist, thinker, or the like. **musings, musers.** *v.* **3.** To be absorbed in one's thoughts; engage in meditation. **4.** To consider or say thoughtfully. **mused, musing.** *adj.* **mused. 5.** Perplexed, bewildered, bemused. **musing. 6.** Being absorbed in thoughts; reflecting deeply; contemplating; engaged in meditation. **muse-lipped.**

mutable Capable of or subject to change or alteration.

mutation ('s) An alteration or change, as in nature, form, or quality. **mutations.**

mutilated Having a part of the body crippled or disabled; disfigured; damaged, marred.

muzzle The forward, projecting part of the head of certain animals, such as dogs, including the mouth, nose, and jaws; the snout.

myrrh An aromatic gum resin obtained from several trees and shrubs of the genus *Commiphora* of India, Arabia, and eastern Africa, used in perfume and incense.

mystic *n.* **1.** One who believes in the existence of realities beyond human comprehension and who has had spiritual experiences. **mystic's.** *adj.* **2.** Of occult character, power, or significance. **3.** Of the nature of or pertaining to mysteries known only to the initiated; esoteric. **4.** Having an import not apparent to the senses nor obvious to the intelligence; beyond ordinary understanding.

Sri Aurobindo: "I used the word 'mystic' in the sense of a certain kind of inner seeing and feeling of things, a way which to the intellect would seem occult and visionary -- for this is something different from imagination and its work with which the intellect is familiar." *On Himself*

"The mystic feels real and present, even ever present to his experience, intimate to his being, truths which to the ordinary reader are intellectual abstractions or metaphysical speculations." *Letters on Savitri*

"To the mystic there is no such thing as an abstraction. Everything which to the intellectual mind is abstract has a concreteness, substantiality which is more real than the sensible form of an object or of a physical event." *Letters on Savitri*

mystique An aura of mystery or mystical power surrounding a person, object, concept or pursuit.

nascent Coming into existence; emerging.

nave The central part of a church.

nescience Absence of knowledge or awareness; ignorance. **nescient.**

Sri Aurobindo: "Nescience in Nature is the complete self-ignorance; . . . ." *The Life Divine*

nether 1. Dwelling beneath the surface of the earth. **2.** Lower or under.

niche A recess in a wall, as for holding a statue or urn.

night-repairs Resorts or haunts of the night.

No-gestures The gestures or movements of a classical drama of Japan, with music and dance performed in a highly stylised manner by elaborately dressed performers on an almost bare stage.

no man's land 1. An unowned or unclaimed tract of usually barren land. **2.** An area between opposing armies, over which no control has been established.

No-man's-land.

Sri Aurobindo: "As to the two lines with 'no man's land' there can be no capital in the first line because there it is a description while the capital is needed in the other line, because the phrase has acquired there the force of a name or appellation. I am not sure about the hyphen; it could be put but the no hyphen might be better as it suggests that no one in particular has as yet got possession." *Letters on Savitri.*

Non-Being   Sri Aurobindo: "Non-Being is only a word. When we examine the fact it represents, we can no longer be sure that absolute non-existence has any better chance than the infinite Self of being more than an ideative formation of the mind. We really mean by this Nothing something beyond the last term to which we can reduce our purest conception and our most abstract or subtle experience of actual being as we know or conceive it while in this universe. This Nothing then is merely a something beyond positive conception. And when we say that out of Non-Being Being appeared, we perceive that we are speaking in terms of Time about that which is beyond Time." *The Life Divine*

Non-Being's, Non-being's, non-being, non-being's,

nook   Any remote or sheltered spot; any small corner or recess.

nostalgia   A bittersweet longing for things, persons, or situations of the past.

nuptial   Of or relating to marriage or the wedding ceremony. Also *fig.*

nymphs   *Greek & Roman Mythology*: Any of numerous minor deities represented as beautiful maidens inhabiting and sometimes personifying features of nature such as trees, waters, and mountains.

oblivious   **1.** Without remembrance or memory. **2.** Unmindful; unconscious; unaware (usually followed by *of*).

obscured   *adj.* **1.** Made unclear, vague, or hidden to the sight. *v.* **2.** Made less visible or unclear; concealed. **obscuring.**

occult   **1.** Hidden from view; concealed. **2.** Beyond the realm of human comprehension; inscrutable. **3.** Available only to the initiate; secret.

Sri Aurobindo: "The ancient knowledge in all countries was full of the search after the hidden truths of our being and it created that large field of practice and inquiry which goes in Europe by the name of occultism, -- we do not use any corresponding word in the East, because these things do not seem to us so remote, mysterious and abnormal as to the occidental mentality; they are nearer to us and the veil between our normal material life and this larger life is much thinner." *The Synthesis of Yoga*

". . . a true occultism means no more than a research into supraphysical realities and an unveiling of the hidden laws of being and Nature, of all that is not obvious on the surface. It attempts the discovery of the secret laws of mind and mental energy, the secret laws of life and life-energy, the secret laws of the subtle-physical and its energies, -- all that Nature has not put into visible operation on the surface; it pursues also the application of these hidden truths and powers of Nature so as to extend the mastery of the human spirit beyond the ordinary operations of mind, the ordinary operations of life, the ordinary operations of our physical existence. In the spiritual domain which is occult to the surface mind in so far as it passes beyond normal and enters into supernormal experience, there is possible not only the discovery of the self and spirit, but the discovery of the uplifting, informing and guiding light of spiritual consciousness and the power of the spirit, the spiritual way of knowledge, the spiritual way of action. To know these things and to bring their truths and forces into the life of humanity is a necessary part of its evolution. Science itself is in its own way an occultism; for it brings to light the formulas which Nature has hidden and it uses its knowledge to set free operations of her energies which she has not included in her ordinary operations and to organise and place at the service of man her occult powers and processes, a vast system of physical magic, -- for there is and can be no other magic than the utilisation of secret truths of being, secret powers and processes of Nature. It may even be found that a supraphysical knowledge is necessary for the completion of physical knowledge, because the processes of physical Nature have behind them a supraphysical factor, a power and action mental, vital or spiritual which is not tangible to any outer means of knowledge." *The Life Divine.*

occultist   One who is versed in the occult arts.

ode   1. A lyric poem of some length, usually of a serious or meditative nature and having an elevated style and formal stanzaic structure. **2.** A poem meant to be sung. **odes.**

oestrus   A regularly occurring period of sexual receptivity in most female mammals, except humans, during which ovulation occurs and copulation can take place; heat. [from Latin *oestrus* gadfly, hence frenzy, from Greek *oistros*]

ominous 1. Of or being an omen, especially an evil one. **2.** Foreboding evil.

omnipotent 1. Having absolute, unlimited power. **the Omnipotent. 2.** An epithet for God. **Omnipotent's.**

Sri Aurobindo: "One seated in the sleep of Superconscience, a massed Intelligence, blissful and the enjoyer of Bliss.... This is the omnipotent, this is the omniscient, this is the inner control, this is the source of all." *The Upanishads*

"By self-realisation of Brahman as our self we find the force, the divine energy which lifts us beyond the limitation, weakness, darkness, sorrow, all-pervading death of our mortal existence; by the knowledge of the one Brahman in all beings and in all the various movement of the cosmos we attain beyond these things to the infinity, the omnipotent being, the omniscient light, the pure beatitude of that divine existence." *The Upanishads*

omniscience 1. The state of being omniscient; having infinite knowledge. **2.** Universal or infinite knowledge. **Omniscience. 3.** God.

Sri Aurobindo: "Mind is not sufficient to explain existence in the universe. Infinite Consciousness must first translate itself into infinite faculty of Knowledge or, as we call it from our point of view, omniscience." *The Life Divine*

omniscient 1. Having total knowledge; knowing everything. **2.** One having total knowledge. **3. Omniscient** God. Used with *the.* **Omniscient.**

Sri Aurobindo: "The omniscient is not born, nor dies, nor has he come into being from anywhere, nor is he anyone. He is unborn, he is constant and eternal, he is the Ancient of Days who is not slain in the slaying of the body. . . ." *The Upanishads*

"This is the omniscient who knows the law of our being and is sufficient to his works; let us build the song of his truth by our thought and make it as if a chariot on which he shall mount. When he dwells with us, then a happy wisdom becomes ours. With him for friend we cannot come to harm." *The Secret of the Veda*

Omniscient's.

opulent Rich; sumptuous; luxurious.

oracle 1. A person, such as a priestess, through whom a deity is held to respond when consulted. **2.** The response given through such a medium, often in the form of an enigmatic statement or allegory. **3.** A command or revelation from God. **oracles.**

oracular Of, relating to, or being an oracle.

Overmind Sri Aurobindo: "The overmind is a sort of delegation from the supermind (this is a metaphor only) which supports the present evolutionary universe in which we live here in Matter. If supermind were to start here from the beginning as the direct creative Power, a world of the kind we see now would be impossible; it would have been full of the divine Light from the beginning, there would be no involution in the inconscience of Matter, consequently no gradual striving evolution of consciousness in Matter. A line is therefore drawn between the higher half of the universe of consciousness, parardha , and the lower half, aparardha. The higher half is constituted of Sat, Chit, Ananda, Mahas (the supramental) -- the lower half of mind, life, Matter. This line is the intermediary overmind which, though luminous itself, keeps from us the full indivisible supramental Light, depends on it indeed, but in receiving it, divides, distributes, breaks it up into separated aspects, powers, multiplicities of all kinds, each of which it is possible by a further diminution of consciousness, such as we reach in Mind, to regard as the sole or the chief Truth and all the rest as subordinate or contradictory to it." *Letters on Yoga*

"The overmind is the highest of the planes below the supramental." *Letters on Yoga*

"In its nature and law the Overmind is a delegate of the Supermind Consciousness, its delegate to the Ignorance. Or we might speak of it as a protective double, a screen of dissimilar similarity through which Supermind can act indirectly on an Ignorance whose darkness could not bear or receive the direct impact of a supreme Light." *The Life Divine*

"The Overmind is a principle of cosmic Truth and a vast and endless catholicity is its very spirit; its energy is an all-dynamism as well as a principle of separate dynamisms: it is a sort of inferior Supermind, -- although it is concerned predominantly not with absolutes, but with what might be called the dynamic potentials or pragmatic truths of Reality, or with absolutes mainly for their power of generating pragmatic or creative values, although, too, its comprehension of things is more global than integral, since its totality is built up of global wholes or constituted by separate independent realities uniting or coalescing together, and although the essential unity is grasped by it and felt to be basic of things and pervasive in their manifestation, but no longer as in the Supermind their intimate and ever-present secret, their dominating continent, the overt constant builder of the harmonic whole of their activity and nature." *The Life Divine*

"The overmind sees calmly, steadily, in great masses and large extensions of space and time and relation, globally; it creates and acts in the same way -- it is the world of the great Gods, the divine Creators." *Letters on Yoga*

"The Overmind is essentially a spiritual power. Mind in it surpasses its ordinary self and rises and takes its stand on a spiritual foundation. It embraces beauty and sublimates it; it has an essential aesthesis which is not limited by rules and canons, it sees a universal and an eternal beauty while it takes up and transforms all that is limited and particular. It is besides concerned with things other than beauty or aesthetics. It is concerned especially with truth and knowledge or rather with a wisdom that exceeds what we call knowledge; its truth goes beyond truth of fact and truth of thought, even the higher thought which is the first spiritual range of the thinker. It has the truth of spiritual thought, spiritual feeling, spiritual sense and at its highest the truth that comes by the most intimate spiritual touch or by identity. Ultimately, truth and beauty come together and coincide, but in between there is a difference. Overmind in all its dealings puts truth first; it brings out the essential truth (and truths) in things and also its infinite possibilities; it brings out even the truth that lies behind falsehood and error; it brings out the truth of the Inconscient and the truth of the Superconscient and all that lies in between. When it speaks through poetry, this remains its first

essential quality; a limited aesthetical artistic aim is not its purpose."
Letters on Savitri

"In the overmind the Truth of supermind which is whole and harmonious
enters into a separation into parts, many truths fronting each other and
moved each to fulfil itself, to make a world of its own or else to prevail or
take its share in worlds made of a combination of various separated Truths
and Truth-forces." *Letters on Yoga*

Overmind's.

overseers Those who survey or watch, as from a higher position.

pactise Sri Aurobindo combines the word *pact* [an agreement or
covenant] with *ise*, a noun suffix occurring in loanwords from French,
indicating quality, condition, or function.

palpable **1.** Capable of being handled, touched, or felt; tangible. **2.**
Readily or plainly seen, heard, perceived, etc.; obvious; evident.

parable **1.** A short allegorical story designed to illustrate or teach some
truth, spiritual principle, or moral lesson. **2.** A statement or comment
that conveys a meaning indirectly by the use of comparison, analogy, or
the like, *esp.* concerning morality or ethics.

parley A discussion, discourse, or conference.

passion *n.* **1.** Suffering. **2.** A powerful emotion, such as love, joy, hatred,
or anger. **3.** An abandoned display of emotion, especially of anger. **4.**
Strong sexual desire; lust. **5.** Violent anger. **6.** The sufferings of Jesus
in the period following the Last Supper and including the Crucifixion, as
related in the New Testament. **passion's, passions, world-passion.**
adj. **passioning.** *v.* **7.** To be affected by intense emotions such as love,
joy, hatred, anger, etc. **passions, passioned, passioning, passion-
tranced.**

pavilions Elaborate and decorative structures or other buildings
connected to a larger building; annexes.

pell-mell *n.* **1.** A confused mixture or crowd, a medley. *adv.* **2.** In
frantic disorderly haste; headlong.

peopled Furnished with or as if with people; populated. Also *fig.* **high-peopled.**

percept 1. A mental impression of something perceived by the senses, viewed as the basic component in the formation of concepts; a sense datum. **2.** The act of perceiving; an impression or sensation of something perceived.

perilous 1. Full of or involving peril; dangerous. **2.** Fraught with danger.

peripheries 1. Outside boundaries or surfaces of things. **2.** The outermost boundaries of an area.

perplexed Filled with confusion or bewilderment; puzzled; troubled. **perplexing.**

perspective 1. A visible scene, *esp.* one extended to a distance; vista. **2.** The appearance of things relative to one another as determined by their distance from the viewer. **3.** A mental view or outlook. **perspectives.**

perturb To disturb greatly; make uneasy or anxious. **perturbed, perturbing.**

peter out To diminish gradually and stop; dwindle to nothing.

petrified Made rigid or inert; hardened; deadened.

Phalanx An Ancient Military Formation Of Serried Ranks Surrounded By Shields; Hence, Any Crowded Mass Of People Or Group United For A Common Purpose. **Phalanxes, Phalanxed.**

phenomenon 1. An unusual, significant, or unaccountable fact or occurrence; a marvel. **2.** *Phil.* An object as it is perceived by the senses.

photon The quantum of electromagnetic energy, regarded as a discrete particle having zero mass, no electric charge, and an indefinitely long lifetime. **photon's.**

phrase 1. A characteristic way or mode of expression. **2.** An expression of two or more words in sequence that form a syntactic unit that is less than a complete sentence. **phrases.**

pillared   1. Having pillars. **2.** Made into pillars. Also *fig.* **thousand-pillared.**

planed   Soared or glided.

plash   1. The sound of a light splash. **2.** A gentle splash. **plashing.**

plasm   The protoplasm of the germ cells that contains chromosomes and genes.

plebian

plinth   A block or slab on which a pedestal, column, or statue is placed.

plumbless   Something whose depth cannot be fathomed. Also *fig.*

poignant   1. Piercing; incisive. **2.** Agreeably intense or stimulating. **3.** Sharply distressing or painful to the feelings. **poignancy.**

poise   1. A state of balance or equilibrium; stability. lit. and *fig.* **2.** A dignified, self-confident manner or bearing; composure; self-possession. **3.** A state or condition of hovering or being suspended; suspense or indecision. **poised, self-poised, wide-poised.**

polities   Forms of government of a nation, state, church, or organization.

pomp   1. Dignified or magnificent display; splendour. Also *fig.* **2.** A procession or pageant. **3.** Vain or ostentatious display. **pomps.**

postulates   Things assumed without proof as being self-evident or generally accepted, *esp.* when used as a basis for an argument.

posture   1. A position of the body or of body parts. **2.** One's image or policy as perceived by the public. **3.** A stance or disposition with regard to something. **4.** *Fig.* A frame of mind affecting one's thoughts or behaviour; an overall attitude. **postures.**

potency   1. Efficacy; effectiveness; strength. **2.** Inherent capacity for growth and development; potentiality. **potencies.**

pranked   Dressed or decorated showily or gaudily.

prating   Uttering empty or foolish talk; chattering; babbling.

precarious   1. Dangerously lacking in security or stability. **2.** Subject to chance or unknown conditions.

prescience Knowledge of actions or events before they occur; foresight; foreknowledge. **prescient.**

priest A person whose office it is to perform religious rites, and *esp.* to make sacrificial offerings. **priests, priest-wind's.**

priestly Sacred; characteristic of a priest.

primal **1.** Being first in time; original; primeval. **2.** Of first importance; primary.

primaeval Belonging to the first or earliest age or ages; original or ancient.

proclaim **1.** To announce officially and publicly; declare. **2.** To extol or praise publicly. **proclaims, proclaimed, proclaiming.**

profaning Treating with irreverence, esp. with towards sacred objects.

professions Acts of professing; avowals; promises; declarations.

profound n. **1.** That which is eminently deep, or the deepest part of something; a vast depth; an abyss. lit. and *fig;* chiefly poetical. *adj.* **2.** Situated at or extending to great depth; too deep to have been sounded or plumbed. **3.** Coming as if from the depths of one's being. **4.** Of deep meaning; of great and broadly inclusive significance. **5.** Being or going far beneath what is superficial, external, or obvious. **6.** Showing or requiring great knowledge or understanding. **profounder.**

prompter ('s) **1.** *Theat.* A person offstage who reminds the actors of forgotten lines or cues. **2.** A person, thing, etc., that prompts. **prompters, sprite-prompters.**

prophet **1.** A person who speaks by divine inspiration or as the interpreter through whom the will of a god is expressed. **2.** A person who predicts the future. **prophet's, prophets.** (Sri Aurobindo often employs the word as an adjective.) **prophet-passion, prophet-speech.**

prostrate **1.** Lying face down, as in submission or adoration. **2.** *Fig.* Reduced to extreme weakness or incapacitation; overcome.

protean Readily taking on varied shapes, forms, or meanings.

proton A positively charged elementary particle that is a fundamental constituent of all atomic nuclei.

provisional Providing or serving for the time being only; existing only until permanently or properly replaced; temporary.

prow **1.** The forward part of a ship's hull; the; bow. **2.** A ship. poet.

puny Of inferior size, strength, or significance; weak.

pupilled Became like the pupil of an eye. (Sri Aurobindo employs the word as a v.)

purblind **1.** Slow or deficient in understanding, imagination or vision. **2.** *Fig.* Slow in understanding or discernment; dull.

purveyor A person or thing that habitually provides or supplies a particular thing or quality. **purveyors.**

quarries Open excavations or pits from which stone is obtained by digging, cutting, or blasting.

quarter A place of residence. Also *fig.* **quarters.**

quarter A place of residence. Also *fig.* **quarters.**

quell **1.** To put down forcibly; suppress. **2.** To overcome; suppress or allay. quelled.

quiver n. **1.** The act or state of quivering; a tremble or tremor. quivering, quiverings. v. **2.** To shake with a slight, rapid, tremulous movement *esp.* with emotion. **quivers, quivered, quivering.**

rack *n.* **1.** Torment; anguish. *v.* **2.** To inflict torment and anguish. *adj.* **racked, self-racked.**

railed Enclosed with a bar of wood or metal fixed horizontally for any of various purposes, as for a support, barrier, or fence. Also *fig.* **sense-railed.**

raiment Clothing; garments. **raiment's.**

rapt **1.** Deeply engrossed or absorbed. **2.** Entranced; transported with emotion; enraptured; ecstatic. **3.** Indicating, proceeding from, characterized by, a state of rapture. **4.** Carried off spiritually to another place, sphere of existence, etc. **self-rapt.**

rapturous Filled with great joy or rapture; ecstatic. **rapturously.**

reach *n.* **1.** Range of effective action, power, or capacity, area, sphere, scope. **2.** The range of influence, power, jurisdiction, etc. **reaches.** *v.* **3.** To stretch out or put forth (a body part); extend. **4.** To arrive at or get to (a place, person, etc.) in the course of movement or action. **5.** To arrive at; attain. **6.** To make contact or communication with (someone). **7.** To extend in influence or operation. **reaches, reached, reaching.**

realism The representation in art or literature of objects, actions, or social conditions as they actually are, without idealization or presentation in abstract form.

reason *v.* **1.** To form conclusions, judgments, or inferences from facts or premises. **2.** To determine or conclude by logical thinking. **reasons, reasoned.** *n.* **3.** An underlying fact or cause that provides logical sense for a premise or occurrence. **Reason, reason's, Reason's.**

Sri Aurobindo: "The reason itself is only a special kind of application, made by a surface regulating intelligence, of suggestions which actually come from a concealed, but sometimes partially overt and active power of the intuitive spirit." *The Synthesis of Yoga*

"The characteristic power of the reason in its fullness is a logical movement assuring itself first of all available materials and data by observation and arrangement, then acting upon them for a resultant knowledge gained, assured and enlarged by a first use of the reflective powers, and lastly assuring itself of the correctness of its results by a more careful and formal action, more vigilant, deliberate, severely logical which tests, rejects or confirms them according to certain secure standards and processes developed by reflection and experience." *The Synthesis of Yoga*

"Reason is only a messenger, a representative or a shadow of a greater consciousness beyond itself which does not need to reason because it is all and knows all that it is." *The Life Divine*

". . . reason is in its nature an imperfect light with a large but still restricted mission. . . ." *The Human Cycle*

". . . reason can only establish half-lights and a provisional order." *The Human Cycle*

"Yet in the principle of reason itself there is the assertion of a Transcendence. For reason is in its whole aim and essence the pursuit of Knowledge, the pursuit, that is to say, of Truth by the elimination of error." *The Life Divine*

"Reason, on the contrary, proceeds by analysis and division and assembles its facts to form a whole; but in the assemblage so formed there are opposites, anomalies, logical incompatibilities, and the natural tendency of Reason is to affirm some and to negate others which conflict with its chosen conclusions so that it may form a flawlessly logical system." *The Life Divine.*

regent One who governs as or in place of a king or queen; a ruler.

regurgitations Movements of rushing or surging back.

relief Alleviation, ease, or deliverance through the removal of pain, distress, oppression, etc.

relief 1. Projection of a figure or part from the ground or plane on which it is formed, as in sculpture or similar work. **2.** Prominence, distinctness or vividness of outline due to contrast of colour.

rendezvous A prearranged meeting place.

renounce 1. To give up (a title, for example), *esp.* by formal announcement. **2.** To reject; disown; disclaim; refuse to recognize. **3.** To give up or put aside voluntarily; forsake, forego, forswear. **renounces, renounced, renouncing.**

repatriate To restore or return to the country of birth, citizenship, or origin. Also *fig.*

reveal 1. To make known (something concealed or secret) **2.** To lay open to view; to uncover as if drawing away a veil. **reveals, revealed,**

revealing, all-revealing, new-revealed, self-revealed, self-revealing.

reverie **1.** A state of dreamy meditation or fanciful musing. **2.** A daydream. **reverie's, reveries.**

rhythmic Cadenced; rhythmical.

Rider, the superhuman **Kalki**

Sri Aurobindo: "Avatarhood would have little meaning if it were not connected with the evolution. The Hindu procession of the ten Avatars is itself, as it were, a parable of evolution. First the Fish Avatar, then the amphibious animal between land and water, then the land animal, then the Man-Lion Avatar, bridging man and animal, then man as dwarf, small and undeveloped and physical but containing in himself the godhead and taking possession of existence, then the rajasic, sattwic, nirguna Avatars, leading the human development from the vital rajasic to the sattwic mental man and again the overmental superman. Krishna, Buddha and Kalki depict the last three stages, the stages of the spiritual development -- Krishna opens the possibility of overmind, Buddha tries to shoot beyond to the supreme liberation but that liberation is still negative, not returning upon earth to complete positively the evolution; Kalki is to correct this by bringing the Kingdom of the Divine upon earth, destroying the opposing Asura forces. The progression is striking and unmistakable." *Letters on Yoga*

"No system indeed by its own force can bring about the change that humanity really needs; for that can only come by its growth into the firmly realised possibilities of its own higher nature, and this growth depends on an inner and not an outer change. But outer changes may at least prepare favourable conditions for that more real amelioration, -- or on the contrary they may lead to such conditions that the sword of Kalki can alone purify the earth from the burden of an obstinately Asuric humanity. The choice lies with the race itself; for as it sows, so shall it reap the fruit of its Karma." *The Human Cycle*

rift A gap or space made by cleaving or splitting; a fissure or cleft, as in an opening or break in a forest, clouds or mist. **rifts.**

ritual   *n.* **1.** The prescribed order of a religious ceremony. **2.** Any practice or pattern of behaviour regularly performed in a set manner. *adj.* **3.** Of the nature of or practiced as a rite or ritual.

sack The plundering of a captured place; pillage; looting. sacrament **1.** Something regarded as possessing a sacred or mysterious significance. **2.** A rite believed to be a means of or visible form of grace. **3.** A sign, token or symbol. **4.** A pledge. **sacraments.**

sacrifice   *n.* **1.** The surrender to God or a deity, for the purpose of propitiation or homage, of some object of possession. Also applied *fig.* to the offering of prayer, thanksgiving, penitence, submission, or the like. **2.** Forfeiture or surrender of something highly valued for the sake of one considered to have a greater value or claim. **tree-of-sacrifice.** *v.* **3.** To surrender or give up (something).

Sri Aurobindo: "Sacrifice means an inner offering to the Divine and the real spiritual sacrifice is a very joyful thing." *Letters on Yoga*

"The true essence of sacrifice is not self-immolation, it is self-giving; its object not self-effacement, but self-fulfilment; its method not self-mortification, but a greater life, not self-mutilation, but a transformation of our natural human parts into divine members, not self-torture, but a passage from a lesser satisfaction to a greater Ananda." *The Synthesis of Yoga*

"In the spiritual sense, however, sacrifice has a different meaning -- it does not so much indicate giving up what is held dear as an offering of oneself, one's being, one's mind, heart, will, body, life, actions to the Divine. It has the original sense of 'making sacred' and is used as an equivalent of the word *yajna*. When the Gita speaks of the 'sacrifice of knowledge', it does not mean a giving up of anything, but a turning of the mind towards the Divine in the search for knowledge and an offering of oneself through it. It is in this sense, too, that one speaks of the offering or sacrifice of works. The Mother has written somewhere that the spiritual sacrifice is joyful and not painful in its nature. On the spiritual path, very commonly, if a seeker still feels the old ties and responsibilities strongly he is not asked to sever or leave them, but to let the call in him grow till all within is ready. Many, indeed, come away earlier because they feel that to cut loose is their only chance, and these have to go sometimes through a struggle. But the pain, the struggle, is not the essential character of this spiritual self-offering." *Letters on Yoga*

satellite 1. One who attends a powerful dignitary; a subordinate. **2.** A small body in orbit around a larger body. **satellites.**

Satyavan "Son of King Dyumatsena; the tale of Satyavan and Savitri is told in the *Mahabharata* as a story of conjugal love conquering death." *Glossary and Index of Proper Names in Sri Aurobindo's Works*

Sri Aurobindo: "Satyavan is the soul carrying the divine truth of being within itself but descended into the grip of death and ignorance; . . ." (Author's note at the preface to *Savitri.*)

"He the Eternal's delegate soul in man." *Savitri* 10. 3.

". . . the soul of the world called Satyavan

Freed from thy clutch of pain and ignorance

That he may stand master of life and fate,

Man's representative in the house of God,

The mate of Wisdom and the spouse of Light,

The eternal bridegroom of the eternal bride." *Savitri,* 10. 4.

Satyavan's.

satyr *Class. Myth.* One of a class of woodland deities, attendant on Bacchus, represented as part human, part horse, and sometimes part goat, and noted for riotousness and lasciviousness. **satyr's.**

Savitri "In the *Mahabharata*, the heroine of the tale of Satyavan and Savitri; . . . . She was the daughter of King Ashwapati, and lover of Satyavan, whom she married although she was warned by Narada that he had only one year to live. On the fatal day, when Yama carried off Satyavan's spirit, she followed him with unswerving devotion. Ultimately Yama was constrained to restore her husband to life." *Glossary and Index of Proper Names in Sri Aurobindo's Works*

Sri Aurobindo: "Savitri is the Divine Word, daughter of the Sun, goddess of the supreme Truth who comes down and is born to save; . . . ." (Author's note at beginning of *Savitri*.)

"Savitri is represented in the poem as an incarnation of the Divine Mother . . . ." *Letters on Savitri*

The Mother: "Savitri [the poem] is a mantra for the transformation of the world." *Spoken to Udar*

Savitri's.

savour   **1.** A specific taste or smell. *v.* **2.** To derive or receive pleasure from; get enjoyment from; take pleasure in. **savoured**

scanted   Made limited; stinted.

schema   A diagrammatic representation; an outline or model.

scornful   Full of scorn, contemptuous, derisive.

scourge   *n.* **1.** A whip used to inflict punishment. **2.** A cause of affliction or calamity. *v.* **3.** To punish severely; whip; flog. **4.** To chastise severely.

scourged   Beaten, flogged.

seer   **1.** A person gifted with profound spiritual insight or knowledge; a wise person or sage who possesses intuitive powers or one to whom divine revelations are made in visions. **2.** One who sees; an observer. **Seer, seers, seer-evenings, seer-summit, seer-vision's.**

Sri Aurobindo: "The seer does not need the aid of thought in its process as a means of knowledge, but only as a means of representation and expression, -- thought is to him a lesser power and used for a secondary purpose. If a further extension of knowledge is required, he can come at it by new seeing without the slower thought processes that are the staff of support of the mental search and its feeling out for truth, -- even as we scrutinise with the eye to find what escaped our first observation" *The Synthesis of Yoga*

The Seer, the Thinker, the Self-existent who becomes everywhere has ordered perfectly all things from years sempiternal. *Isha Upanishad.* (1) *The Life Divine*

"This supreme Soul and Self is the Seer, the Ancient of Days and in his eternal self-vision and wisdom the Master and Ruler of all existence who sets in their place in his being all things that are, ..." *Essays on the Gita*

"It is He that has gone abroad -- That which is bright, bodi-less, without scar of imperfection, without sinews, pure, unpierced by evil. The Seer, the Thinker,(1) the One who becomes everywhere, the Self-existent has ordered objects perfectly according to their nature from years sempiternal." *The Upanishads*

"There is a clear distinction in Vedic thought between *kavi*, the seer and *manîshî*, the thinker. The former indicates the divine supra-intellectual Knowledge which by direct vision and illumination sees the reality, the principles and the forms of things in their true relations, the latter, the labouring mentality, which works from the divided consciousness through the possibilities of things downward to the actual manifestation in form and upward to their reality in the self-existent Brahman." *The Upanishads*

semblance 1. An appearance or likeness; a resemblance to something or someone similar. **2.** An outward token or appearance, *esp.* without any inner substance or reality. **semblances, half-semblances.**

sentient Having the power of sense perception or sensation; conscious.

sentinel 1. A tower used by the military to watch for the enemy and defend a camp, etc. **2.** A person or thing that watches or stands as if watching. **3.** A soldier stationed as a guard to challenge all comers and prevent a surprise attack; a sentry. (Sri Aurobindo often employs the word as an adjective.) **sentinels.**

Sequent Following in order or succession.

seraglios The harem of a Muslim house or palace; a place in a Sultan's palace where concubines and wives are secluded. Also *fig.*

seraph A member of the highest order of angels, often represented as a child's head with wings above, below, and on each side. (Sri Aurobindo also employs the word as an *adj.*) **seraph's, seraph-winged.**

serf A member of the lowest feudal class, attached to the land owned by a lord and required to perform labor in return for certain legal or customary rights; one in bondage or servitude.

servile Submissive; slavish; fawning; slave-like.

sever **1.** To separate (a part) from the whole as by cutting or the like. **2.** To divide or be divided suddenly or forcibly; to break up; cleave. **3.** To become separated from each other. **severed, severing.**

Shalwa "In the *Mahabarata*, name of a country in western India; also the name of its king or its people." *(Dow.) Glossary and Index of Proper Names in Sri Aurobindo's Works*

sheen **1.** Lustre, brightness, radiance. **2.** Splendid attire. **dawn-sheen.**

shepherd *n.* **1.** In combination, denoting a thing such as is used by or is characteristic of shepherds, as a shepherd's staff. **shepherd's. 2.** One who protects, guides, or watches over a person or group of people. *Fig.* a spiritual guardian. (Sri Aurobindo employs the word in this sense as an *adj.*) *v.* **3.** To tend, watch over carefully, guard or guide as a shepherd does his sheep. **shepherds.**

sieged Assailed or assaulted; besieged.

simulacrum An image or representation of something; *esp.*, a slight, unreal, or vague semblance of something; superficial likeness.

siren *Classical Mythol.* One of several fabulous sea nymphs, part woman, part bird, who were supposed to lure sailors to destruction by their enchanting singing. *Fig.* One who, or that which, sings sweetly, charms, allures, or deceives, like the Sirens. (Sri Aurobindo uses the word in its adjectival sense: Seductive, tempting.)

sleight A clever or skilful trick or deception; an artifice or stratagem.

slumbrous **1.** Sleepy; heavy with drowsiness, as the eyelids. **2.** Peaceful; tranquil. **3.** Inactive or sluggish; calm or quiet.

sojourner A temporary resident; a visitor.

solace *n.* **1.** Comfort in sorrow, misfortune, or distress; consolation. *v.* **2.** To comfort, cheer, or console, as in trouble or sorrow. **3.** To allay, alleviate, assuage, soothe. **solaced.**

solemn 1. Performed, executed, or associated with religious ceremony. **2.** Characterized by dignified or serious formality, as proceedings; of a formal or ceremonious character. **3.** Grave or sober, as a person, the face, speech, tone, or mood. **4.** Gravely or sombrely impressive; causing serious thoughts or a grave mood.

solicited Approached with entreaty or petition, for, or to do, something; urged, importuned; asked earnestly or persistently.

somnolence A state of drowsiness; sleepiness.

sorcery The use of supernatural power over others through the assistance of spirit; witchcraft. **sorceries.**

sordid 1. Morally ignoble or base; vile, *esp.* moved by meanly selfish motives. **2.** Unrefined; coarse; unpolished. **sordid-thoughted.**

sovereign *n.* **1.** One that exercises supreme, permanent authority, as a king, queen or monarch. Often applied to the Divine. **child-sovereign.** *adj.* **2.** Supreme; pre-eminent; indisputable. **3.** Being above all others in character, importance, excellence, etc. **4.** Having supreme rank, power or authority. **5.** Belonging to or characteristic of a king, queen or other supreme ruler; royal, regal, majestic.

specious 1. Having the ring of truth or plausibility but actually false. **2.** Apparently good or right thought lacking real merit; superficially pleasing or plausible. **3.** Plausible but false.

sprite-prompters Elves, fairies, or goblins that incite, or move others, often against their will.

spume *n.* **1.** Foam or froth on a liquid, as on the sea. *v.* **2. spumed.** Foamed or frothed.

spurned Rejected disdainfully or contemptuously; scorned.

squadrons Armoured cavalry units.

squalid   Dirty and repulsive, *esp.* as a result of neglect or poverty; filthy.

stade   A period or stage in a journey.

stalk   **1.** To pursue or approach prey, quarry, etc., stealthily. **2.** To walk with a stiff, haughty, or angry gait. **stalked.**

stanza   One of the divisions of a poem, composed of two or more lines usually characterized by a common pattern of meter, rhyme, and number of lines. **stanzas.**

staple   A basic or necessary item of food.

start   *n.* **1.** A beginning of an action, journey, series of events, etc. **2.** An initial but often transient display of energy at the onset of an activity. **3.** A sudden involuntary jerking movement of the body. **starts.** *v.* **4.** To begin or set out, as on a journey or activity. **5.** To appear or come suddenly into action, life, view, etc.; rise or issue suddenly forth. **starts, started, starting.**

station   **1.** A place or position where a person or thing stands or is assigned to stand; a post. **2.** Social position; rank **stations.**

statuesque   Like or suggesting a statue, as in massive or majestic dignity, grace, or beauty. **statuesques.** (Sri Aurobindo employs the word as a *v.*)

storeyed   Having storeys, divided into storeys. **many-storeyed.** (Modern spelling: *storied*)

stupendous   Of astounding force, volume, degree, or excellence; marvelous.

subconscient   Sri Aurobindo: "In our yoga we mean by the subconscient that quite submerged part of our being in which there is no wakingly conscious and coherent thought, will or feeling or organised reaction, but which yet receives obscurely the impressions of all things and stores them up in itself and from it too all sorts of stimuli, of persistent habitual movements, crudely repeated or disguised in strange forms can surge up into dream or into the waking nature. No, subliminal is a general term used for all parts of the being which are not on the waking surface. Subconscient is very often used in the same sense by European psychologists because they do not know the difference. But when I use the word, I mean always what is *below* the ordinary physical consciousness, not what is behind it. The inner mental, vital, physical, the psychic are not subconscious in this sense, but they can be spoken of as subliminal." *The Synthesis of Yoga.*

"The subconscient is a concealed and unexpressed inarticulate consciousness which works below all our conscious physical activities. Just as what we call the superconscient is really a higher consciousness above from which things descend into the being, so the subconscient is below the body-consciousness and things come up into the physical, the vital and the mind-nature from there.

Just as the higher consciousness is superconscient to us and supports all our spiritual possibilities and nature, so the subconscient is the basis of our material being and supports all that comes up in the physical nature." *Letters on Yoga*

"That part of us which we can strictly call subconscient because it is below the level of mind and conscious life, inferior and obscure, covers the purely physical and vital elements of our constitution of bodily being, unmentalised, unobserved by the mind, uncontrolled by it in their action. It can be held to include the dumb occult consciousness, dynamic but not sensed by us, which operates in the cells and nerves and all the corporeal stuff and adjusts their life process and automatic responses. It covers also those lowest functionings of submerged sense-mind which are more operative in the animal and in plant life." *The Life Divine*

"The subconscient is a thing of habits and memories and repeats persistently or whenever it can old suppressed reactions, reflexes, mental, vital or physical responses. It must be trained by a still more persistent insistence of the higher parts of the being to give up its old responses and take on the new and true ones." *Letters on Yoga*

"About the subconscient -- it is the sub-mental base of the being and is made up of impressions, instincts, habitual movements that are stored there. Whatever movement is impressed in it, it keeps. If one impresses the right movement in it, it will keep and send up that. That is why it has to be cleared of old movements before there can be a permanent and total change in the nature. When the higher consciousness is once established in the waking parts, it goes down into the subconscient and changes that also, makes a bedrock of itself there also." *Letters on Yoga*

"The sub-conscious is the evolutionary basis in us, it is not the whole of our hidden nature, nor is it the whole origin of what we are. But things can rise from the subconscient and take shape in the conscious parts and much of our smaller vital and physical instincts, movements, habits, character-forms has this source." *Letters on Yoga*

"The subconscient is the support of habitual action -- it can support good habits as well as bad." *Letters on Yoga*

"For the subconscient is the Inconscient in the process of becoming conscious; it is a support and even a root of our inferior parts of being and their movements." *The Life Divine* **subconscient's.**

sublimity Something in physical objects that evokes or awakens awe and reverence.

suit A group of things used together; a set or collection; a sequence.

sullen **1.** Sombre; gloomy; dismal; sluggish; slow. **2.** Gloomy or sombre in tone, color, or portent. Chiefly *poet.*

sumptuous **1.** Rich and superior in quality. **2.** Magnificent; splendid. **3.** Luxuriously fine or large; lavish; splendid.

superconscient Sri Aurobindo: ". . . the superconscient is consciousness taken up into an absolute of being." *The Life Divine*

Superconscient, superconscient's, Superconscient's.

superfluity Overabundance or excess in the most positive sense.

superhuman **1.** Exceeding normal human ability or experience. **2.** Above or beyond the human; preternatural or supernatural. **superhuman's.**

supermind Sri Aurobindo: "The Supermind is the total Truth-Consciousness; the Overmind draws down the truths separately and gives them a separate activity -- e.g. in the Supermind the Divine Peace and Power, Knowledge and Will are one. In the Overmind each of these becomes a separate aspect which can exist or act on its own lines apart from the others.

It is the cryptic verses of the Veda that help us here; for they contain, though concealed, the gospel of the divine and immortal Supermind and through the veil some illumining flashes come to us. We can see through these utterances the conception of this Supermind as a vastness beyond the ordinary firmaments of our consciousness in which truth of being is luminously one with all that expresses it and assures inevitably truth of vision, formulation, arrangement, word, act and movement and therefore truth also of result of movement, result of action and expression, infallible ordinance or law. Vast all-comprehensiveness; luminous truth and harmony of being in that vastness and not a vague chaos or self-lost obscurity; truth of law and act and knowledge expressive of that harmonious truth of being: these seem to be the essential terms of the Vedic description." *The Life Divine*

"By the supermind is meant the full Truth-Consciousness of the Divine Nature in which there can be no place for the principle of division and ignorance; it is always a full light and knowledge superior to all mental substance or mental movement." *Letters on Yoga*

"The Supermind is in its very essence a truth-consciousness, a consciousness always free from the Ignorance which is the foundation of our present natural or evolutionary existence and from which nature in us is trying to arrive at self-knowledge and world-knowledge and a right consciousness and the right use of our existence in the universe. The Supermind, because it is a truth-consciousness, has this knowledge inherent in it and this power of true existence; its course is straight and can go direct to its aim, its field is wide and can even be made illimitable. This is because its very nature is knowledge: it has not to acquire knowledge but possesses it in its own right; its steps are not from nescience or ignorance into some imperfect light, but from truth to greater truth, from right perception to deeper perception, from intuition to intuition, from illumination to utter and boundless luminousness, from growing widenesses to the utter vasts and to very infinitude. On its summits it possesses the divine omniscience and omnipotence, but even in an evolutionary movement of its own graded self-manifestation by which it would eventually reveal its own highest heights it must be in its very nature essentially free from ignorance and error: it starts from truth and light and moves always in truth and light. As its knowledge is always true, so too its will is always true; it does not fumble in its handling of things or stumble in its paces. In the Supermind feeling and emotion do not depart from their truth, make no slips or mistakes, do not swerve from the right and the real, cannot misuse beauty and delight or twist away from a divine rectitude. In the Supermind sense cannot mislead or deviate into the grossnesses which are here its natural imperfections and the cause of reproach, distrust and misuse by our ignorance. Even an incomplete statement made by the Supermind is a truth leading to a further truth, its incomplete action a step towards completeness." *The Supramental Manifestation*

"Supermind is the grade of existence beyond mind, life and Matter and, as mind, life and Matter have manifested on the earth, so too must Supermind in the inevitable course of things manifest in this world of Matter. In fact, a supermind is already here but it is involved, concealed behind this manifest mind, life and Matter and not yet acting overtly or in its own power: if it acts, it is through these inferior powers and modified by their characters and so not yet recognisable. It is only by the approach and arrival of the descending Supermind that it can be liberated upon earth and reveal itself in the action of our material, vital and mental parts so that these lower powers can become portions of a total divinised activity of our whole being: it is that that will bring to us a completely realised divinity or the divine life." *Essays in Philosophy and Yoga*

"The supermind is the vast Truth-Consciousness of which the ancient seers spoke; there have been glimpses of it till now, sometimes an indirect influence or pressure, but it has not been brought down into the consciousness of the earth and fixed there. To so bring it down is the aim of our yoga." *Letters on Yoga*

"The essential character of Supermind is a Truth-consciousness which knows by its own inherent right of nature, by its own light: it has not to arrive at knowledge but possesses it." *Essays in Philosophy and Yoga*

Supermind, supermind's.

supernal 1. Belonging to the realm or state above this world or this present life; pertaining to a higher world or state of existence; coming from above; belonging to the heaven of divine beings; heavenly, celestial, or divine. **2.** Lofty; of more than earthly or human excellence, powers, etc. **supernal's.**

Sri Aurobindo: "In the ancient Indian system there is only one triune supernal, Sachidananda. Or if you speak of the upper hemisphere as the supernal, there are three, Sat plane, Chit plane and Ananda plane. The Supermind could be added as a fourth, as it draws upon the other three and belongs to the supper hemisphere." *Letters on Yoga and On Himself*

suppressed 1. Kept from being revealed, published, circulated, or voiced. **2.** Kept in; repressed; subdued; inhibited.

surreal Having the hallucinatory quality of a dream; unreal; fantastic.

swaddled Wrapped or bound in bandages; swathed.

swathes Formations such as those of clouds, or mists that appear to envelope something.

sway *n.* **1.** Power; dominant influence. **2.** Dominion or control; sovereign command. **3.** The act of moving from side to side with a swinging motion. *v.* **4.** To cause to swing back and forth or to and fro. **5.** To cause to incline or bend to one side. **sways, swayed, swaying.**

sylvan 1. Of, pertaining to, or inhabiting the woods. **2.** Consisting of or abounding in woods or trees; wooded.

tabernacle 1. Any place or house of worship. **2.** A temple, often the human body as a dwelling place for the soul.

tawny Of a dark yellowish or dull yellowish-brown colour.

Te Deums   Ancient liturgical hymns, literally: "Thee, God, we praise"; a service of thanksgiving in which the recital of this hymn forms a central part.

tenebrous   Dark and gloomy.

tenement   *Fig.* A building for human habitation, often in reference to the soul in the body.

tented   Settled or lodged as in a tent; encamped.

tenuous   **1.** Diluted or rarefied in consistency or density. **2.** *Fig.* Insignificant or flimsy.

terrain   *n.* **1.** An area of land; ground. Also *fig.* **terrains.** *adj.* **2.** Of the earth, *esp.* with reference to its physical character.

thaumaturge   A performer of miracles. **Thaumaturge, thaumaturgist.**

theorem   **1.** A rule or law *esp.* one expressed by an equation or formula. **2.** An idea that has been demonstrated as true or is assumed to be so demonstrable.

theoricians   Those who hold theories; theorists.

throb   *n.* **1.** The act of throbbing; a beating, palpitation, or vibration. **2.** Any pulsation or vibration. **3.** A strong rhythmic vibration or beat. **throbs, heart-throb, wave-throbs.** *v.* **4.** To beat strongly or with increased force or rapidity, as the heart under the influence of emotion or excitement; palpitate. **throbs, throbbed.**

thyrsus   *Greek myth.* A staff, usually one tipped with a pine cone, borne by Dionysus (Bacchus) and his followers.

tinge   *n.* **1.** A trace, or slight amount, most of as of a colour. Also *fig. v.* **2.** To apply a trace of color to; tint. **3.** To affect as in thought or feeling. **tinged, tinging, fire-tinged, many-tinged.**

titan   **1.** One of prodigious size, strength, or achievement. **2.** Gigantic, immense.

topaz   A highly valued precious stone, transparent and lustrous, usually of a deep yellow but occasionally other colours.

tour-de-force   An exceptional achievement; a masterly or brilliant stroke, creation, effect, or accomplishment.

tract   An expanse of land or water. **tracts, tract-memories, flower-tracts.**

tranced   Hypnotic or ecstatic. Also *fig.* **passion-tranced.**

transcendent   Surpassing others; preeminent or supreme.

transience   The attribute of being brief or fleeting; impermanence.

transient 1. Passing with time; transitory. **2.** Remaining in a place only a brief time.

translate 1. To transfer from one place or condition to another. **2.** To express or be capable of being expressed in another language or dialect. **3.** To put into simpler terms; explain or interpret. **4.** To change from one form, function, or state to another; convert or transform. **translates, translated, translating.**

transmute   To change from one nature, substance, form, or condition into another; transform; convert. **transmutes, transmuted, transmuting, transmutingly.**

tremulous 1. Marked by trembling, quivering, or shaking. **2.** Timid, timorous, fearful.

triple heavens   Sri Aurobindo: "Vishnu is the wide-moving one. He is that which has gone abroad -- as it is put in the language of the Isha Upanishad, *sa paryag*ât, -- triply extending himself as Seer, Thinker and Former, in the superconscient Bliss, in the heaven of mind, in the earth of the physical consciousness, *tredhâ vicakramânah.* In those three strides he has measured out, he has formed in all their extension the earthly worlds; for in the Vedic idea the material world which we inhabit is only one of several steps leading to and supporting the vital and mental worlds beyond. In those strides he supports upon the earth and mid-world, -- the earth the material, the mid-world the vital realms of Vayu, Lord of the dynamic Life-principle, -- the triple heaven and its three luminous summits, *trîni rocanâ.* These heavens the Rishi describes as the higher seat of the fulfilling. Earth, the mid-world and heaven are the triple place of the conscious being's progressive self-fulfilling, *trishadhastha*, earth the lower seat, the vital world the middle, heaven the higher. All these are contained in the threefold movement of Vishnu." *The Secret of the Veda*

triple mystic heaven

triumphant 1. Victorious; conquering. **2.** Triumphal.

troll A supernatural creature of Scandinavian folklore, variously portrayed as a friendly or mischievous dwarf or as a giant, that lives in caves, in the hills, or under bridges. **trolls, troll-like.**

trudge A long tiring or exhausting walk.

truth 1. *(Often cap.)* Ideal or fundamental reality apart from and transcending perceived experience. **2.** Conformity to fact or actuality. **Truth, truth's, Truth's, truths, Truths, truth-conscious, Truth-gaze, Truth-speaking, All-Truth, dream-truth, half-Truth, half-truths, heaven-truth, soul-truth.**

Sri Aurobindo: "Science started on the assumption that the ultimate truth must be physical and objective -- and the objective Ultimate (or even less than that) would explain all subjective phenomena. Yoga proceeds on the opposite view that the ultimate Truth is spiritual and subjective and it is in that ultimate Light that we must view objective phenomena." *Letters on Yoga*

"The supreme truths are neither the rigid conclusions of logical reasoning nor the affirmations of credal statement but fruits of the soul's inner experience. Intellectual truth is only one of the doors to the outer precincts of the temple." *The Foundations of Indian Culture*

". . . Truth is the secret of life and power . . . ." *The Human Cycle*

The Mother: "The Truth is something living, moving, expressing itself at each second, and it is one way of approaching the Supreme." *Collected Works of the Mother, Vol. 15.*

"The Truth is not linear but global: it is not successive but simultaneous. Therefore it cannot be expressed in words: it has to be lived." *Collected Works of the Mother, Vol. 15.*

"Truth is a difficult and strenuous conquest. One must be a real warrior to make this conquest, a warrior who fears nothing, neither enemies nor death, for with or against everybody, with or without a body, the struggle continues and will end by Victory." *Collected Works of the Mother, Vol. 15.*

Truth-Consciousness   Sri Aurobindo: "The Truth-Consciousness is everywhere present in the universe as an ordering self-knowledge by which the One manifests the harmonies of its infinite potential multiplicity." *The Life Divine*

"The intermediate link exists. We call it the Supermind or the Truth-Consciousness, because it is a principle superior to mentality and exists, acts and proceeds in the fundamental truth and unity of things and not like the mind in their appearances and phenomenal divisions." *The Life Divine*

"A supramental Truth-Consciousness is at once the self-awareness of the Infinite and Eternal and a power of self-determination inherent in that self-awareness;" *The Life Divine*

"For the supermind is a Truth-Consciousness in which the Divine Reality, fully manifested, no longer works with the instrumentation of the Ignorance; a truth of status of being which is absolute becomes dynamic in a truth of energy and activity of the being which is self-existent and perfect. Every movement there is a movement of the self-aware truth of Divine Being and every part is in entire harmony with the whole. Even the most limited and finite action is in the Truth-Consciousness a movement of the Eternal and Infinite and partakes of the inherent absoluteness and perfection of the Eternal and Infinite." *The Synthesis of Yoga*

"The mind is ignorance seeking for the Truth, the supramental by its very definition is the Truth-Consciousness, Truth in possession of itself and fulfilling itself by its own power." *Letters on Yoga*

"The supramental is simply the Truth-Consciousness and what it brings in its descent is the full truth of life, the full truth of consciousness in Matter. One has indeed to rise to high summits to reach it, but the more one rises, the more one can bring down below." *Letters on Yoga*

"By a Truth-consciousness is meant -- a Knowledge consciousness which is immediately, inherently and directly aware of Truth in manifestation and has not to seek for it like Mind." **truth-consciousness.** *Letters on Yoga*

tumult **1.** Violent and noisy commotion or disturbance of a crowd or mob; uproar. **2.** A disorderly commotion or disturbance. **3.** Great emotional or mental agitation. **tumults.**

'twas Contraction of it was.

twixt Contraction of *betwixt*; between.

unappeased Not pacified; unsatisfied.

undertone **1.** A low or subdued tone. **2.** An underlying tone (of feeling, etc.); a subordinate or unobtrusive quality or element; an undercurrent. **undertones.**

unerring **1.** Undeviatingly accurate throughout; not containing any error or flaw. **2.** Making no error or mistake; not going or leading astray in judgement or opinion. **3.** Not going astray from the intended mark; certain, sure. **unerringly.**

unhedged Not enclosed with or as with a hedge.

unquenched Unextinguished; unsuppressed.

unwont Not wont, used, or accustomed to do something.

usurp To seize or obtain possession of (territory, land, etc.) in an unjust or illegal manner; to assume unjust rule, dominion, or authority over, to appropriate wrongfully. **usurped.**

vagrancy The state of wandering from place to place; having no permanent home.

vanity **1.** Excessive pride in one's appearance, qualities, abilities, achievements, etc.; character or quality of being vain; conceit; an instance or display of this quality or feeling. **2.** Lack of usefulness, worth, or effect; worthlessness.

vanquished Defeated or overcome; subdued. **half-vanquished.** (Sri Aurobindo also employs the word as a *n.*)

vastitudes 1. The condition or quality of being vast. **2.** A vast space, expanse, extent, etc.

velamen *Anat.* A membranous covering; velum. **velamen's.**

verge 1. The extreme edge or margin; a border. **2.** An enclosing limit, line, belt, or strip. **3.** The edge of something as the horizon, mainly *poetic.* **4.** The limit beyond which something happens or changes. **verge's, verges.**

veridical 1. Truthful; veracious. **2.** Real; actual; genuine.

verities Something, such as a statement, principle, or belief, that is true, especially an enduring truth.

vermilion A brilliant scarlet red.

vessel 1. A hollow or concave utensil, as a cup, bowl, pitcher, or vase, used for holding liquids or other contents. Also *fig.* **2.** A person regarded as a holder or receiver of something; *esp.* something nonmaterial. **vessels.**

vibrant 1. Pulsating with vigour and energy. **2.** Vigorous; energetic; vital. **3.** Characterized by or exhibiting vibration; pulsating or trembling. **4.** Exhibiting or characterized by rapid, rhythmic movement back and forth or to and fro; vibrating.

vicegerent Invested with or characterised by delegated authority.

vicissitudes 1. Successive, alternating, or changing phases or conditions, as of life or fortune. **2.** Changes or variations occurring in the course of something.

vied vie. To strive in competition or rivalry with another; to contend for superiority. **vying.**

vigil A watch kept during normal sleeping hours. **Vigil.**

vigilant Keenly watchful to detect danger; wary.

vindicate To provide justification or support for. **vindicated.**

Virat "(Purusha) The universal or cosmic Soul; 'God practical'; Lord of Waking-Life, who governs, preserves and maintains the sensible creation which Hiranyagarbha has shaped." *Glossary and Index of Proper Names in Sri Aurobindo's Works*

Sri Aurobindo: "The Self that becomes all these forms of things is the Virat or universal Soul; the Self that creates all these forms is Hiranyagarbha, the luminous or creatively perceptive Soul." *The Synthesis of Yoga*

"These two sets of three names each mean the same things. Visva or Virat=the Spirit of the external universe, Hiranyagarbha or Taijasa (the Luminous)=the Spirit in the inner planes, Prajna or Ishwara=the Superconscient Spirit, Master of all things and the highest Self on which all depends." *Letters on Yoga*

". . . Virat, the seer and creator of gross forms, ..." *The Future Poetry*

virtue 1. The quality of doing what is right and avoiding what is wrong. **2.** Moral excellence; goodness; righteousness. **3.** A particular moral excellence; a good or admirable quality or property. An example or kind of moral excellence. **virtues.**

visage 1. The face, usually with reference to features, expression, etc.; countenance. **2.** Aspect; appearance. **visages.**

familiar visage. Sri Aurobindo [in reference to the following lines]:

Often, a familiar visage studying.

His vision warned by the spirit's inward eye

Discovered suddenly Hell's trademark there.

"It is a reference to the beings met in the vital world, that seem like human beings but, if one looks closely, they are seen to be Hostiles; often assuming the appearance of a familiar face they try to tempt or attack by surprise, and betray the stamp of their origin — there is also a hint that on earth too they take up human bodies or possess them for their own purpose." *Letters on Savitri*

voluptuous **1.** Giving, characterized by, or suggesting ample, unrestrained pleasure to the senses. **2.** Sensuously pleasing or delightful. **voluptuously.**

wallowings Acts or instances of rolling around in water, mud or filth. Also *fig.*

wards Divisions or districts of a city or town.

weft 1. The horizontal threads interlaced through the warp in a woven fabric; woof. **2.** Something woven, like fabric. Also *fig.* **marvel-wefts, wonder-weft.**

weltering Rolling, tossing, or tumbling about as or as if by the sea, waves, or wind; raging, surging.

whorls Forms that coils or spiral; curls or swirls.

wizard

wizened

wood-nymphs Nymphs of the woods; dryads.

Writhen Twisted; contorted

wry

zeal

zenith

CPSIA information can be obtained at www.ICGtesting.com
Printed in the USA
LVOW07s2111280515

440297LV00004B/441/P